NICOTEXT

ANIMALISTICUS FANTASTICUS

Copyright © NICOTEXT 2010 All rights reserved.
NICOTEXT part of Cladd media ltd.
www.nicotext.com
info@nicotext.com

Printed in Poland
ISBN: 978-91-86283-05-6

MOUSE LEMURS ARE
THE SMALLEST PRIMATES IN THE WORLD.

A 1,200 POUND (540 KG) HORSE EATS ABOUT
SEVEN TIMES ITS OWN WEIGHT EACH YEAR.

ELECTRIC LIGHT OR LIGHT FROM YOUR TV SET
WILL MAKE A CAT SHED ITS FUR.

A BIRD REQUIRES MORE FOOD IN PROPORTION
TO ITS SIZE THAN A HUMAN BABY OR A CAT.

ACCORDING TO EXPERTS, WHALE SONGS RHYME.

A CAPON IS A CASTRATED ROOSTER.

A GROUP OF HERRING IS CALLED A SIEGE.
A GROUP OF JELLYFISH IS CALLED A SMACK.

A CHAMELEON CAN MOVE ITS EYES IN TWO
DIRECTIONS AT THE SAME TIME.

ANIMAL GESTATION PERIODS: THE SHORTEST
IS THE AMERICAN OPOSSUM, WHICH BEARS
ITS YOUNG 12-13 DAYS AFTER CONCEPTION;
THE LONGEST IS THE ASIATIC ELEPHANT,
TAKING 608 DAYS, OR JUST
OVER 20 MONTHS.

A CHAMELEON'S TONGUE IS TWICE
THE LENGTH OF ITS BODY.

A MALE SEA CATFISH KEEPS THE EGGS OF HIS
YOUNG IN HIS MOUTH UNTIL THEY ARE READY TO
HATCH. HE WILL NOT EAT UNTIL THEY ARE BORN,
WHICH MAY TAKE SEVERAL WEEKS.

A CHIMPANZEE CAN LEARN TO RECOGNIZE
ITSELF IN A MIRROR, BUT MONKEYS CAN'T.

AUSTRALIAN TERMITES HAVE BEEN KNOWN
TO BUILD MOUNDS 20 FT (6 M) HIGH AND AT
LEAST 100 FT (30 M) WIDE.

A CORNISH GAME HEN IS REALLY A YOUNG
CHICKEN, USUALLY 5-6 WEEKS OF AGE THAT
WEIGHS NO MORE THAN 2 LBS (0.9 KG).

THE STUFF THAT PEOPLE ARE ALLERGIC TO
(ALLERGENS) IN CATS IS A PROTEIN IN CAT
SALIVA. WHEN THE CAT GROOMS AND THE
SALIVA DRIES IT CAN BECOME AIRBORNE.
THIS PROTEIN IS 1/3 THE WEIGHT OF ORDINARY
HOUSE DUST, SO IT CAN TRAVEL FARTHER.
YOU CAN EVEN FIND THIS ALLERGEN
WHERE CATS HAVE NEVER BEEN.

A COW PRODUCES NEARLY 200,000 GLASSES OF MILK IN HER LIFETIME.

A MALE EMPEROR PENGUIN WITHSTANDS THE ANTARCTIC COLD FOR 60 DAYS OR MORE TO PROTECT HIS EGGS, WHICH HE KEEPS ON HIS FEET, COVERED WITH A FEATHERED FLAP. DURING THIS ENTIRE TIME HE DOESN'T EAT A THING. MOST MALE PENGUINS LOSE ABOUT 25 LBS (11 KG) WHILE THEY WAIT FOR THEIR BABIES TO HATCH. WHEN THEY FINALLY EMERGE THEY FEED THE CHICKS A SPECIAL LIQUID FROM THEIR THROATS. ONLY WHEN THE FEMALE PENGUINS RETURN TO CARE FOR THE YOUNG, DO THE FATHERS GO TO SEA TO EAT AND REST.

MANY FISH CAN CHANGE SEX DURING THE
COURSE OF THEIR LIVES. OTHERS, ESPECIALLY
RARE DEEP SEA FISH, HAVE BOTH MALE
AND FEMALE SEX ORGANS.

OVER 100 MILLION BIRDS A YEAR
DIE FROM SMASHING INTO WINDOWS IN
NORTH AMERICA ALONE.

GIRAFFES CAN CLEAN THEIR EARS WITH
THEIR HALF METER (1.6 FT) LONG TONGUE.

A FEMALE MACKEREL LAYS ABOUT 500,000
EGGS AT ONCE.

A DRAGONFLY CAN SPOT AN INSECT
MOVING 33 FT (10 M) AWAY.

A HINDU TEMPLE DEDICATED TO THE RAT
GODDESS KARNI MATA IN DESHNOKE, INDIA,
HOUSES MORE THAN 20,000 RATS.

FEMALE FLEAS CONSUME FIFTEEN TIMES
THEIR WEIGHT DAILY.

A HOLSTEIN COW'S SPOTS ARE LIKE A FINGER-
PRINT OR SNOWFLAKE. NO TWO COWS HAVE
EXACTLY THE SAME PATTERN OF SPOTS.

THE HYDRA - A CLOSE RELATIVE OF JELLYFISH
AND SEA ANEMONES, CAN REGENERATE OR
GROW BACK IF IT IS CUT IN HALF.

A LEECH IS A WORM THAT FEEDS ON BLOOD.
IT WILL PIERCE ITS VICTIM'S SKIN, FILL ITSELF
WITH THREE TO FOUR TIMES ITS OWN BODY
WEIGHT IN BLOOD, AND WILL NOT FEED
AGAIN FOR MONTHS.

MOST ELEPHANTS WEIGH LESS THAN THE
TONGUE OF A BLUE WHALE.

A NEWBORN KANGAROO IS ABOUT 1 INCH
(24.5 MM) IN LENGTH.

GIANT TORTOISES OF THE GALAPAGOS ISLANDS
WEIGH UP TO 500 LBS (225 KG) AND CAN
LIVE FOR OVER 150 YEARS.

A COW'S STOMACH HAS FOUR COMPARTMENTS:
THE RUMEN (WHERE MICROBES ARE FERMENT-
ED), THE RECTICULUM (STORAGE AREA), THE
OMASUM (WHERE WATER IS ABSORBED), AND
THE ABOMASUM (THE ONLY COMPARTMENT
WITH DIGESTIVE JUICES).

THE FEMALE LION IS A MUCH MORE EFFICIENT
HUNTER THAN THE MALE.

A POLECAT ISN'T REALLY A CAT.
IT IS A NOCTURNAL EUROPEAN WEASEL.

A LARGE SWARM OF LOCUSTS CAN EAT
180 000 LBS (80 TONS) OF CORN IN A DAY.

A QUARTER OF ALL HORSES IN THE U.S. DIED
OF A VAST VIRUS EPIDEMIC IN 1872.

AS A GENERAL RULE IN THE ANIMAL KINGDOM:
THE MORE COMPLEX OR RELATIVELY BIG THE
EYES ARE IN RELATION TO THE BODY,
THE SMALLER THE BRAIN IS.

A RAT CAN LAST LONGER WITHOUT
WATER THAN A CAMEL.

THE BIGGEST SHARK SPECIES HAS THE
SMALLEST TEETH. THE 40 FT (12 M) LONG WHALE
SHARK HAS MORE THAN 4,000 TEETH,
EACH ONLY 0.01 FT (3 MM) LONG.

A SINGLE LITTLE BROWN BAT CAN CATCH 1200
MOSQUITO-SIZED INSECTS IN JUST ONE HOUR.

AN ELEPHANT HERD CAN MOVE
50 MILES (80 KM) IN ONE DAY.

A WOODPECKER CAN PECK
TWENTY TIMES A SECOND.

BATS ALWAYS TURN LEFT
WHEN LEAVING A CAVE.

A ZEBRA IS WHITE WITH
BLACK STRIPES.

GREAT WHITE SHARKS CAN GO AS LONG AS
THREE MONTHS WITHOUT EATING.

AFTER MATING, THE MALE SURINAM TOAD
AFFIXES THE FEMALE'S EGGS TO HER BACK,
WHERE HER SPONGY FLESH WILL SWELL AND
ENVELOPE THEM. WHEN THE TADPOLES HATCH,
THEY LEAVE BEHIND HOLES IN THEIR MOTHER'S
FLESH THAT THEY WILL REMAIN SHELTERED
IN UNTIL LARGE ENOUGH TO FEND
FOR THEMSELVES.

MAYFLIES LIVE FOR A YEAR OR MORE AS LARVA;
BUT AS ADULTS THEY LIVE FOR ONLY
A FEW HOURS.

ALL CLAMS START OUT AS MALES;
SOME CHANGE INTO FEMALES AT
SOME POINT IN THEIR LIVES.

THE LARVA OF THE POLYPHEMUS MOTH
CONSUMES 86,000 TIMES ITS BIRTH
WEIGHT IN ITS FIRST 56 DAYS.

ALL PET HAMSTERS ARE DESCENDED FROM A
SINGLE FEMALE WILD GOLDEN HAMSTER
FOUND WITH A LITTER OF 12 YOUNG
IN SYRIA IN 1930.

ACCORDING TO ONE STUDY, PLANT AND ANIMAL
SPECIES ARE BECOMING EXTINCT AT THE RATE
OF 17 SPECIES PER HOUR.

AN ADULT LION'S ROAR CAN BE HEARD UP
TO 5 MILES (8 KM) AWAY, AND WARNS OFF
INTRUDERS OR REUNITES SCATTERED
MEMBERS OF THE PRIDE.

BY SWALLOWING WATER, THE PUFFERFISH
BECOMES TOO BIG FOR OTHER FISH
TO SWALLOW.

AN ALBATROSS CAN SLEEP WHILE IT FLIES.
IT APPARENTLY DOZES WHILE CRUISING
AT 25 MPH (40 KM/H).

TICKS ARE SECOND ONLY TO THE MOSQUITO
AS THE MOST DANGEROUS PARASITES
TO HUMANS.

AN ELECTRIC EEL CAN PRODUCE
A SHOCK OF UP TO 650 VOLTS.

THE WINGSPAN OF THE INDONESIAN FRUIT
BAT EQUALS THE HEIGHT OF FILM
STAR SYLVESTER STALLONE.

AN IGUANA CAN STAY UNDER
WATER FOR 28 MINUTES.

THE COMMON BLACK ANTS AND WOOD ANTS
HAVE NO STING, BUT THEY CAN SQUIRT A SPRAY
OF FORMIC ACID. SOME BIRDS PUT ANTS IN
THEIR FEATHERS BECAUSE THE ANTS
SQUIRT FORMIC ACID, WHICH GETS
RID OF PARASITES.

AN OSTRICH'S EYE IS BIGGER
THAN ITS BRAIN.

A DRAGONFLY HAS A LIFESPAN
OF 24 HOURS.

ANCIENT EGYPTIANS BELIEVED THAT THE
GODDESS BAST WAS THE MOTHER OF ALL CATS
ON EARTH. THEY ALSO BELIEVED THAT
CATS WERE SACRED ANIMALS.

WE SHARE 98.4% OF OUR DNA WITH
A CHIMP - AND 70% WITH A SLUG.

POLAR BEARS ARE THE ONLY MAMMAL WITH
HAIR ON THE SOLES OF THEIR FEET.

AT NEARLY 50% FAT, WHALE MILK HAS AROUND
10 TIMES THE FAT CONTENT OF HUMAN MILK,
WHICH HELPS CALVES ACHIEVE SOME
SERIOUS GROWTH SPURTS - AS MUCH
AS 200 LBS (90 KG) PER DAY.

SOME MALE SONGBIRDS SING MORE
THAN 2,000 TIMES EACH DAY.

AT THE END OF THE BEATLES' SONG "A DAY IN
THE LIFE," AN ULTRASONIC WHISTLE, AUDIBLE
ONLY TO DOGS, WAS RECORDED BY PAUL
MCCARTNEY FOR HIS SHETLAND SHEEPDOG.

MOSQUITOES ARE ATTRACTED TO THE
COLOR BLUE TWICE AS MUCH AS
TO ANY OTHER COLOR.

BEAVER TEETH ARE SO SHARP THAT NATIVE
AMERICANS USED THEM AS
KNIFE BLADES.

A FEMALE OYSTER, OVER HER LIFETIME, MAY
PRODUCE OVER 100 MILLION YOUNG.

BETWEEN 260 AND 300 MILLION TURKEYS
ARE SLAUGHTERED ANNUALLY IN THE U.S,
ACCORDING TO USDA STATISTICS. OF THESE,
APPROXIMATELY 45 MILLION ARE KILLED
FOR THANKSGIVING, AND 22 MILLION ARE
KILLED FOR CHRISTMAS.

COWS DO NOT HAVE UPPER FRONT TEETH.

BIRD EGGS COME IN A WIDE VARIETY OF SIZES.
THE LARGEST EGG FROM A LIVING BIRD
BELONGS TO THE OSTRICH. IT IS MORE THAN
2,000 TIMES LARGER THAN THE SMALLEST
BIRD EGG, WHICH IS PRODUCED BY THE
HUMMINGBIRD. OSTRICH EGGS ARE ABOUT 7.1"
(18 CM) LONG, 5.5" (14 CM) WIDE AND TYPICALLY
WEIGH 2.7 LBS (0.9 KG). HUMMINGBIRD EGGS
ARE HALF AN INCH LONG (12.7 MM), A THIRD OF
AN INCH (8.5 MM) WIDE AND WEIGH HALF
A GRAM, OR LESS THAN 1/55 OF AN OUNCE.

CAMEL MILK DOESN'T CURDLE.

THE FRUIT FLY'S DNA SEQUENCE IS
180 MILLION BASES LONG,
WHILE A HUMAN'S IS THREE BILLION.

BROWN EGGS COME FROM HENS WITH RED
FEATHERS AND RED EAR LOBES; WHITE EGGS
COME FROM HENS WITH WHITE FEATHERS AND
WHITE EAR LOBES. SHELL COLOR IS DETER-
MINED BY THE BREED OF HEN AND HAS NO
EFFECT ON ITS QUALITY, NUTRIENTS OR FLAVOR.

LOBSTERS CAN LIVE UP TO 50 YEARS.

BIRDS DO NOT SLEEP IN THEIR NESTS.
THEY MAY OCCASIONALLY NAP IN THEM,
BUT THEY ACTUALLY SLEEP IN
OTHER PLACES.

CAMELS HAVE THREE EYELIDS TO PROTECT
THEMSELVES FROM BLOWING SAND.

BUTTERFLIES TASTE WITH
THEIR HIND FEET.

CARNIVOROUS ANIMALS WILL NOT EAT
ANOTHER ANIMAL THAT HAS BEEN
HIT BY A LIGHTNING STRIKE.

CAT SCRATCH DISEASE, A BENIGN BUT SOME-
TIMES PAINFUL DISEASE OF SHORT DURATION,
IS CAUSED BY A BACILLUS. DESPITE ITS NAME,
THE DISEASE CAN BE TRANSMITTED BY MANY
KINDS OF SCRATCHES BESIDES THOSE OF CATS.

CHICKENS ABSORB VITAMIN D FROM
SUNSHINE THROUGH THEIR COMBS.

CATFISH HAVE 100,000 TASTE BUDS.

ABOUT 600 SPECIES OF PLANTS ARE
CARNIVOROUS. MOST EAT INSECTS BUT ALSO
ON THE MENU ARE FROGS, BIRDS AND
EVEN SMALL MONKEYS.

CATNIP CAN AFFECT LIONS AND TIGERS AS
WELL AS HOUSE CATS. IT EXCITES THEM
BECAUSE IT CONTAINS A CHEMICAL THAT
RESEMBLES AN EXCRETION OF THE
DOMINANT FEMALE'S URINE.

THE ONLY DOG IN THE WORLD THAT CAN'T BARK
IS THE BASENJI, AN AFRICAN WOLF DOG.

CERTAIN FROGS CAN BE FROZEN SOLID THEN
THAWED AND CONTINUE LIVING.

WHITE CATS WITH BLUE EYES
ARE USUALLY DEAF.

CHEETAHS MAKE A CHIRPING SOUND THAT IS MUCH LIKE A BIRD'S CHIRP OR A DOG'S YELP. THE SOUND IS SO INTENSE, IT CAN BE HEARD A MILE (1.6 KM) AWAY.

FORTY PERCENT OF ALL CATS ARE AMBIDEXTROUS. THE OTHER 60% ARE EITHER "RIGHT-PAWED" OR "LEFT-PAWED."

COJO, THE FIRST GORILLA BORN IN CAPTIVITY, WAS BORN AT THE COLUMBUS ZOO, IN OHIO, IN 1956 AND WEIGHED 3 1/4 LBS (1.5 KG).

SMALL DOGS USUALLY LIVE LONGER
THAN LARGER BREEDS.

CROCODILES SWALLOW LARGE STONES THAT
STAY PERMANENTLY IN THEIR BELLIES.
IT'S BEEN SUGGESTED THAT THESE
ARE USED FOR BALLAST IN DIVING.

ELEPHANTS ARE THE ONLY ANIMALS
THAT CAN'T JUMP.

DESPITE ITS REPUTATION FOR BEING FINICKY,
THE AVERAGE CAT CONSUMES ABOUT 127,750
CALORIES A YEAR, NEARLY 28 TIMES ITS OWN
WEIGHT IN FOOD AND THE SAME AMOUNT AGAIN
IN LIQUIDS. IN CASE YOU WERE WONDERING,
CATS CAN'T SURVIVE ON A VEGETARIAN DIET.

ELEPHANTS CAN COMMUNICATE USING SOUNDS
THAT ARE BELOW THE HUMAN HEARING RANGE:
BETWEEN 14 AND 35 HERTZ.

YOU ARE MORE LIKELY TO BE KILLED
BY A CHAMPAGNE CORK THAN BY
A POISONOUS SPIDER.

DEVELOPED IN EGYPT ABOUT 5,000 YEARS AGO,
THE GREYHOUND BREED WAS KNOWN BEFORE
THE NINTH CENTURY IN ENGLAND, WHERE IT
WAS BRED BY ARISTOCRATS TO HUNT
SUCH SMALL GAME AS HARES.

A CROCODILE CAN'T STICK ITS TONGUE OUT.

DOLPHINS SLEEP AT NIGHT JUST BELOW THE
SURFACE OF THE WATER. THEY FREQUENTLY
RISE TO THE SURFACE FOR AIR.

A PURRING CAT DOESN'T ALWAYS MEAN A
CONTENTED CAT. CATS WILL ALSO PURR
IF THEY ARE IN PAIN.

DOMESTICATED TURKEYS (FARM RAISED) CAN'T
FLY. WILD TURKEYS CAN FLY FOR SHORT
DISTANCES AT UP TO 55 MPH (90 KM/H).
WILD TURKEYS ARE ALSO FAST ON THE GROUND,
RUNNING AT SPEEDS UP TO 25 MPH (40 KM/H).

THE LEECH HAS 32 BRAINS.

CATS CAN GET BORED. THEY SHOW THEIR
BOREDOM BY EXCESSIVE LICKING,
CHEWING, OR BITING.

DURING WORLD WAR II, THE VERY FIRST BOMB
DROPPED ON BERLIN BY THE ALLIES KILLED
THE ONLY ELEPHANT IN THE BERLIN ZOO.

POLAR BEARS CAN SWIM 60 MILES (97 KM)
WITHOUT PAUSING FOR A REST.

ELEPHANT TUSKS GROW THROUGHOUT AN
ELEPHANT'S LIFE AND CAN WEIGH MORE THAN
200 LBS (90 KG). AMONG ASIAN ELEPHANTS,
ONLY THE MALES HAVE TUSKS. BOTH SEXES
OF AFRICAN ELEPHANTS HAVE TUSKS.

FOR EVERY PERSON THERE ARE ROUGHLY
200 MILLION INSECTS.

IF YOU LIFT A KANGAROO'S TAIL OFF THE
GROUND IT CAN'T HOP – THEY USE THEIR
TAILS FOR BALANCE.

ON AVERAGE, PEOPLE FEAR SPIDERS
MORE THAN THEY DO DEATH.

SOME LIONS MATE OVER 50 TIMES A DAY.

EVERY YEAR, 1.5 BILLION DOLLARS IS SPENT
ON PET FOOD IN THE US. THIS IS FOUR TIMES
THE AMOUNT SPENT ON BABY FOOD.

WHEN TWO DOGS APPROACH EACH OTHER,
THE DOG THAT WAGS ITS TAIL THE
SLOWEST IS IN CHARGE.

FELIX THE CAT IS THE FIRST CARTOON
CHARACTER TO EVER HAVE BEEN MADE IT
INTO A BALLOON FOR A PARADE.

A PANDA'S DIET IS 99% BAMBOO.

FEMALE CHICKENS, OR HENS, NEED ABOUT 24-26
HOURS TO PRODUCE ONE EGG. THIRTY MINUTES
LATER THEY START THE PROCESS ALL OVER
AGAIN. IN ADDITION TO THE HALF HOUR RESTS,
SOME HENS REST EVERY 3-5 DAYS AND
OTHERS REST EVERY 10 DAYS.

CURRENT DOMESTIC CATS WERE THE RESULT
OF GENETIC MUTATION TO MAKE THEM
TAME AT BIRTH.

GEORGE WASHINGTON'S FAVORITE HORSE WAS
NAMED LEXINGTON. NAPOLEON'S FAVOURITE
WAS MARENGO. U.S. GRANT HAD THREE
FAVOURITE HORSES: EGYPT, CINCINNATI,
AND JEFF DAVIS.

GERMAN SHEPHERDS BITE HUMANS MORE
THAN ANY OTHER BREED OF DOG.

THE AVERAGE COW PRODUCES 40
GLASSES OF MILK EACH DAY.

GOLDFISH LOSE THEIR COLOR IF THEY ARE
KEPT IN DIM LIGHT OR ARE PLACED IN A BODY
OF RUNNING WATER, SUCH AS A STREAM.

A HIPPO RUNS FASTER THAN A HUMAN.

HIPPOS HAVE KILLED MORE
THAN 400 PEOPLE IN AFRICA
- MORE THAN ANY OTHER WILD ANIMAL.

CAT WHISKERS ARE FOUND ON THE FACE
AND ON THE BACK OF THE FORELEGS AS WELL.

AS OF 2001, THERE ARE AROUND 44 MILLION
SHEEP IN NEW ZEALAND, A COUNTRY OF
AROUND 4 MILLION PEOPLE.

GREYHOUNDS CAN JUMP A DISTANCE
OF 27 FT (8 M).

HUMMINGBIRDS ARE THE SMALLEST BIRDS
- SO TINY THAT ONE OF THEIR ENEMIES
IS AN INSECT; THE PRAYING MANTIS.

A CHEETAH CAN REACH A TOP SPEED
APPROACHING 70 MPH (113 KM/H).

IN ITS ENTIRE LIFETIME, THE AVERAGE WORKER
BEE PRODUCES 1/12 TEASPOON OF HONEY.

THE FIRST DOG SHOW WAS HELD IN
ENGLAND IN 1859.

INFANT BEAVERS ARE CALLED KITTENS.

IT TAKES 35-65 MINKS TO PRODUCE THE
AVERAGE MINK COAT. THE NUMBERS FOR
OTHER TYPES OF FUR COATS ARE:
BEAVER - 15; FOX - 15 TO 25; ERMINE -
150; CHINCHILLA - 60 TO 100.

GREAT DANES CAN EAT UP TO
8.5 LBS (4 KG) OF FOOD A DAY.

IT TAKES A LOBSTER APPROXIMATELY SEVEN YEARS TO GROW TO BE 1 LB (0.45 KG).

THE TALLEST DOG ON RECORD WAS NAMED SHAMGRET DANZAS. HE WAS 42" (1.06 M) TALL (AT THE SHOULDER) AND WEIGHED 238 LBS (108 KG).

THE NAME ORANGUTAN (ALSO WRITTEN ORANG-UTAN, ORANG UTAN AND ORANGUTANG) IS DERIVED FROM THE MALAY AND INDONESIAN WORDS 'ORANG' MEANING 'PERSON' AND 'HUTAN' MEANING 'FOREST', THUS 'PERSON OF THE FOREST'.

TO FIGURE OUT YOUR DOG'S "TRUE AGE" IN HUMAN TERMS, COUNT THE FIRST FULL YEAR AS 15 YEARS, THE SECOND FULL YEAR AS 10 YEARS AND ALL THE FOLLOWING YEARS AS 3 YEARS. IN OTHER WORDS, A 4 YEAR OLD DOG WOULD BE: 15+10+3+3+=31 YEARS OLD.

LARGE KANGAROOS COVER MORE THAN 30 FT (9 M) WITH EACH JUMP.

A DOG WAS ONCE THE KING OF NORWAY FOR 3 YEARS DURING THE 11TH CENTURY AD. THE NORWEGIAN KING, ANGRY HIS SUBJECTS ONCE DEPOSED HIM, PUT SAUR ON THE THRONE, DEMANDING THAT HE BE TREATED REGALLY.

LASSIE WAS PLAYED BY SEVERAL MALE DOGS, DESPITE THE FEMALE NAME, BECAUSE MALE COLLIES WERE THOUGHT TO LOOK BETTER ON CAMERA. THE MAIN "ACTOR" WAS NAMED PAL.

THE DALMATIAN IS THE ONLY DOG THAT GETS GOUT.

LIONS ARE THE ONLY TRULY SOCIAL CAT SPECIES, AND USUALLY EVERY FEMALE IN A PRIDE, RANGING FROM 5-30 INDIVIDUALS, IS CLOSELY RELATED.

FLEAS HAVE CHANGED HISTORY. MORE HUMAN DEATHS HAVE BEEN ATTRIBUTED TO FLEAS THAN ALL THE WARS EVER FOUGHT. AS CARRIERS OF THE BUBONIC PLAGUE, FLEAS WERE RESPONSIBLE FOR KILLING ONE THIRD OF THE POPULATION OF EUROPE IN THE 14TH CENTURY.

LOVEBIRDS ARE SMALL PARAKEETS THAT LIVE IN PAIRS. MALE AND FEMALE LOVEBIRDS LOOK ALIKE, BUT MOST OTHER MALE BIRDS HAVE BRIGHTER COLORS THAN THE FEMALES.

SOME RIBBON WORMS WILL EAT THEMSELVES IF THEY CAN'T FIND ANY FOOD.

MACARONI, GENTOO, CHINSTRAP AND
EMPEROR ARE TYPES OF PENGUINS.

NEWFOUNDLAND DOGS ARE STRONG
SWIMMERS DUE TO THEIR
WEBBED FEET.

MOCKINGBIRDS CAN IMITATE ANY SOUND
FROM A SQUEAKING DOOR TO
A CAT MEOWING.

THE BIGGEST ANT COLONY WAS FOUND ON THE ISHIKARI COAST OF HOKKAIDO: 306 MILLION WORKER ANTS AND 1 MILLION QUEENS LIVED IN 45,000 INTERCONNECTED NESTS OVER AN AREA OF 1.7 MI2 (2.7 KM2). A WORKER ANT WILL LIVE FOR UP TO 5 YEARS; WHILE A QUEEN WILL LIVE UP TO 25 YEARS.

MOLE RATS ARE THE ONLY EUSOCIAL VERTEBRATES KNOWN TO MAN. THIS MEANS THAT THESE MAMMALS LIVE IN COLONIES SIMILAR TO THOSE OF ANTS AND TERMITES, WITH A SINGLE FERTILE QUEEN GIVING BIRTH TO NON-REPRODUCTIVE WORKERS AND SOLDIERS. MOLE RATS ARE ALSO FAMOUS FOR THEIR INCREDIBLY POWERFUL JAWS, THE MUSCLES OF WHICH CONSTITUTE 25% OF THEIR BODY MASS. BABY MOLE RATS ARE RAISED ON A DIET OF THEIR OLDER SIBLING'S FECAL PELLETS, EMITTING A SPECIAL CRY WHEN HUNGRY TO SUMMON A WORKER.

ONE IN 5,000 NORTH ATLANTIC LOBSTERS
ARE BORN BRIGHT BLUE.

MOLES ARE ABLE TO TUNNEL THROUGH
300 FT (90 M) OF EARTH IN A DAY.

THE STUDY OF ANTS IS
CALLED MYRMECOLOGY.

OF ALL KNOWN FORMS OF ANIMAL LIFE EVER
TO INHABIT THE EARTH, ONLY ABOUT
10% STILL EXIST TODAY.

THE FROG WAS AN ANCIENT EGYPTIAN SYMBOL,
LATER ADOPTED BY THE CONQUERING ROMANS.
THE FROG-HEADED GODDESS HEKT WAS THE
GODDESS OF BIRTH AND FERTILITY,
AND LATER ALSO OF RESURRECTION.

ON AVERAGE,
PIGS LIVE FOR ABOUT 15 YEARS.

SEXUAL CANNIBALISM, WHERE THE FEMALE
ORGANISM KILLS AND CONSUMES THE MALE OF
THE SAME SPECIES DURING OR AFTER
COPULATION, (RARELY, THESE ROLES ARE
REVERSED) IS COMMON AMONG MANTISES IN
CAPTIVITY, AND UNDER SOME CIRCUMSTANCES
MAY ALSO BE OBSERVED IN THE FIELD.

OWLS HAVE EYEBALLS THAT ARE TUBULAR IN
SHAPE, AND BECAUSE OF THIS, THEY CAN'T
MOVE THEIR EYES.

A FRIGHTENED DOG PUTS ITS TAIL BETWEEN ITS
LEGS BECAUSE IT COVERS THE SCENT GLANDS
IN THE ANAL AREA. SINCE THE ANAL GLANDS
CARRY PERSONAL SCENTS THAT IDENTIFY
INDIVIDUAL DOGS, THE TAIL-BETWEEN-THE-
LEGS BEHAVIOUR IS THE CANINE EQUIVALENT
OF INSECURE HUMANS HIDING THEIR FACES.

PARROTS, MOST FAMOUS OF ALL TALKING
BIRDS, RARELY ACQUIRE A VOCABULARY OF
MORE THAN TWENTY WORDS, HOWEVER
TYMHONEY GREYS AND AFRICAN GREYS HAVE
BEEN KNOWN TO CARRY VOCABULARIES
IN EXCESS OF 100 WORDS.

CATS PREFER TO EAT THEIR FOOD AT 86º F,
WHICH IS WHY THEY DON'T IMMEDIATELY GULP
DOWN THE HALF-EATEN CAN OF FOOD FROM
THE REFRIGERATOR.

PET PARROTS CAN EAT VIRTUALLY ANY COMMON
"PEOPLE-FOOD" EXCEPT FOR CHOCOLATE AND
AVOCADOS. BOTH OF THESE ARE HIGHLY TOXIC
TO THE PARROT AND CAN BE FATAL.

SURVEYS SHOW THAT 62% OF DOG OWNERS
ADMIT THAT THEIR DOG OWNS A SWEATER,
WINTER COAT OR RAINCOAT.

PIGS, WALRUSES AND LIGHT-COLORED
HORSES CAN GET BURNED BY THE SUN.

THE DALMATIAN BREED OF DOG ORIGINATES
FROM THE DALMATIAN COAST OF CROATIA.

PRAIRIE DOGS ARE NOT DOGS.
THEY ARE A KIND OF RODENT.

ACCORDING TO A SURVEY BY THE AMERICAN
ANIMAL HOSPITAL ASSOCIATION, 53% OF PET
OWNERS SPEND THEIR HOLIDAY AND/OR
TRAVEL WITH THEIR PETS.

RATS ARE OMNIVOROUS, EATING NEARLY ANY
TYPE OF FOOD, INCLUDING DEAD AND DYING
MEMBERS OF THEIR OWN SPECIES.

THERE'S A "MEOW" IN THE MIDDLE
OF THE WORD "HOMEOWNER."

RATS CAN'T THROW UP.

SNAILS PRODUCE A COLORLESS, STICKY
DISCHARGE THAT FORMS A PROTECTIVE
CARPET UNDER THEM AS THEY TRAVEL ALONG.
THE DISCHARGE IS SO EFFECTIVE THAT THEY
CAN CRAWL ALONG THE EDGE OF A RAZOR
WITHOUT CUTTING THEMSELVES.

SHARKS APPARENTLY ARE THE ONLY ANIMALS
THAT NEVER GET SICK. AS FAR AS IS KNOWN,
THEY ARE IMMUNE TO EVERY KNOWN
DISEASE – INCLUDING CANCER.

THE SAILFISH, THE SWORDFISH AND THE
MAKO SHARK HAVE ALL BEEN CLOCKED
AT SWIMMING OVER 50 MPH (80 KM/H).

HONEYBEES HAVE HAIR ON THEIR EYES.

ACCORDING TO HOSPITAL FIGURES,
DOGS BITE AN AVERAGE OF 1 MILLION
AMERICANS EACH YEAR.

SNAKES ARE IMMUNE TO THEIR OWN POISON.

THE BIGGEST BIRD IN THE WORLD IS
THE OSTRICH, WHICH CAN GROW UP TO
9 FT (2.7 M) TALL.

SOME BABY GIRAFFES ARE MORE THAN
6 FT (1.8 M) TALL AT BIRTH.

SEA OTTERS USE SO MUCH ENERGY THAT THEY
NEED TO EAT AS MUCH AS ONE THIRD OF
THEIR OWN BODY WEIGHT EACH DAY.

SWANS ARE THE ONLY
BIRDS WITH PENISES.

CERTAIN CHINESE AND AMERICAN ALLIGATORS CAN SURVIVE THE WINTER BY FREEZING THEIR HEADS IN ICE, LEAVING ONLY THEIR NOSE OUT TO BREATH FOR MONTHS ON END.

TAPEWORMS RANGE IN SIZE FROM ABOUT 0.04" (1 MM) TO MORE THAN 50 FT (15 M) IN LENGTH.

THE ALBATROSS HAS A WINGSPAN OF UP TO 14 FT (4 M) AND ONLY NEEDS TO LAND ONCE EVERY COUPLE OF YEARS TO BREED. THEY CAN TRAVEL HUNDREDS OF THOUSANDS OF MILES/ KILOMETERS EACH FLIGHT.

THE "CADUCEUS," THE CLASSICAL MEDICAL
SYMBOL OF TWO SERPENTS WRAPPED AROUND
A STAFF, COMES FROM AN ANCIENT GREEK
LEGEND IN WHICH SNAKES REVEALED THE
PRACTICE OF MEDICINE TO HUMAN BEINGS.

YOU CAN TELL IF A SKUNK IS ABOUT IF YOU
SMELL ONLY 0.000000000000071 OUNCE
OF ITS SPRAY.

THE FIRST BUFFALO EVER BORN IN CAPTIVITY
WAS BORN AT CHICAGO'S LINCOLN PARK
ZOO IN 1884.

WHEN A DOLPHIN IS SICK OR INJURED, ITS
CRIES OF DISTRESS SUMMON IMMEDIATE AID
FROM OTHER DOLPHINS, WHICH TRY TO
SUPPORT IT TO THE SURFACE TO HELP
IT BREATHE.

THE AMERICAN SOCIETY FOR PREVENTION
OF CRUELTY TO ANIMALS (ASPCA) WAS
FORMED IN 1866.

A BEAVER CAN HOLD ITS
BREATH FOR 45 MINUTES.

THE ANACONDA, ONE OF THE WORLD'S LARGEST
SNAKES, GIVES BIRTH TO ITS YOUNG
INSTEAD OF LAYING EGGS.

NO TWO ZEBRAS HAVE THE SAME
STRIPED PATTERN.

THE AVERAGE ADULT MALE OSTRICH,
THE WORLD'S LARGEST LIVING BIRD,
WEIGHS UP TO 345 LBS (156 KG).

FLYING SQUIRRELS DON'T REALLY FLY;
THEY GLIDE FROM BRANCH TO BRANCH.
A BLANKET-LIKE FURRY SKIN STRETCHES
THEIR FRONT AND HIND LEGS, AND ACTS
AS A PARACHUTE, ENABLING THE
SQUIRREL TO SOAR LIKE A KITE.

THE BIGGEST MEMBERS OF THE CAT FAMILY
ARE SIBERIAN AND BENGAL TIGERS, WHICH
CAN REACH OVER 600 LBS (272 KG).

THE GIRAFFE HAS THE HIGHEST
BLOOD PRESSURE OF ANY ANIMAL.

A COMMON MISCONCEPTION IS THAT A LOBSTER SCREAMS WHEN BOILED; THIS IS DUE TO STEAM ESCAPING THE SHELL, CREATING A WHISTLING.

A SCALLOP HAS 35 BLUE EYES.

THE BLOODHOUND IS THE ONLY ANIMAL WHOSE EVIDENCE IS ADMISSIBLE IN AN AMERICAN COURT.

WHEN A HORNED TOAD IS ANGRY, IT SQUIRTS BLOOD FROM ITS EYES.

THE BLUE WHALE IS THE LOUDEST ANIMAL ON EARTH. THE CALL OF THE BLUE WHALE REACHES LEVELS UP TO 188 DECIBELS. THIS EXTRAORDINARILY LOUD WHISTLE CAN BE HEARD FOR HUNDREDS OF MILES/KILOMETERS UNDERWATER.

A SNAIL'S REPRODUCTIVE ORGANS ARE IN ITS HEAD.

THE BONES OF A PIGEON WEIGH
LESS THAN ITS FEATHERS.

MOSQUITOES HAVE
47 TEETH.

A COW'S ONLY SWEAT GLANDS
ARE IN ITS NOSE.

THE CANARY ISLANDS WERE NOT NAMED FOR A
BIRD CALLED A CANARY. THEY WERE NAMED
AFTER A BREED OF LARGE DOGS. THE LATIN
NAME WAS CANARIAE INSULAE
- "ISLAND OF DOGS."

BULLS ARE COLORBLIND.

THE CAT LOVER IS AN AILUROPHILE, WHILE
A CAT HATER IS AN AILUROPHOBE.

JUST ONE COW PRODUCES ENOUGH HARMFUL
METHANE GAS IN A SINGLE DAY TO FILL
AROUND 400 LITRE BOTTLES.

ATTEMPTS HAVE BEEN MADE TO TRAIN ZEBRAS FOR
RIDING SINCE THEY HAVE BETTER RESISTANCE
THAN HORSES TO AFRICAN DISEASES.
HOWEVER MOST OF THESE ATTEMPTS FAILED,
DUE TO THE ZEBRA'S MORE UNPREDICTABLE
NATURE AND TENDENCY TO PANIC UNDER
STRESS. FOR THIS REASON, ZEBRA-MULES
OR ZEBROIDS (CROSSES BETWEEN ANY SPECIES
OF ZEBRA AND A HORSE, PONY, DONKEY OR ASS)
ARE PREFERRED OVER PUREBRED ZEBRAS.

MANY HAMSTERS ONLY BLINK
ONE EYE AT A TIME.

THE CHAMELEON HAS SEVERAL CELL LAYERS
BENEATH ITS TRANSPARENT SKIN. THESE
LAYERS ARE THE SOURCE OF THE CHAMELEON'S
COLOR CHANGE. SOME OF THE LAYERS CONTAIN
PIGMENTS, WHILE OTHERS JUST REFLECT LIGHT
TO CREATE NEW COLORS. SEVERAL FACTORS
CONTRIBUTE TO THE COLOR CHANGE.
A POPULAR MISCONCEPTION IS THAT
CHAMELEONS CHANGE COLOR TO MATCH THEIR
ENVIRONMENT. THIS ISN'T TRUE. LIGHT,
TEMPERATURE, AND EMOTIONAL STATE
COMMONLY BRING ABOUT A CHAMELEON'S
CHANGE IN COLOR. THE CHAMELEON WILL MOST
OFTEN CHANGE BETWEEN GREEN, BROWN AND
GREY, WHICH COINCIDENTLY, OFTEN MATCH THE
BACKGROUND COLORS OF THEIR HABITAT.

GOATS' EYES HAVE RECTANGULAR PUPILS.

THE CHEETAH IS THE ONLY CAT IN THE WORLD
THAT CAN'T RETRACT ITS CLAWS.

GIRAFFES HAVE NO VOCAL CORDS.

THE CHINESE, DURING THE REIGN OF KUBLAI KHAN, USED LIONS ON HUNTING EXPEDITIONS. THEY TRAINED THE BIG CATS TO PURSUE AND DRAG DOWN MASSIVE ANIMALS – FROM WILD BULLS TO BEARS – AND TO STAY WITH THE KILL UNTIL THE HUNTER ARRIVED.

ALL PORCUPINES FLOAT IN WATER.

THE ELEPHANT, AS A SYMBOL OF THE US REPUBLICAN PARTY, WAS ORIGINATED BY CARTOONIST THOMAS NAST AND FIRST PRESENTED IN 1874.

WHEN ANGERED, THE EARS OF TASMANIAN
DEVILS TURN A PINKISH-RED.

THE ENGLISH ROMANTIC POET LORD BYRON
WAS SO DEVASTATED UPON THE DEATH OF HIS
BELOVED NEWFOUNDLAND, WHOSE NAME WAS
BOATSWAIN, THAT HE HAD INSCRIBED UPON THE
DOG'S GRAVESTONE THE FOLLOWING: "BEAUTY
WITHOUT VANITY, STRENGTH WITHOUT
INSOLENCE, COURAGE WITHOUT FEROCITY, AND
ALL THE VIRTUES OF MAN WITHOUT HIS VICES."

HORSES CAN'T VOMIT.

THE EXPRESSION "THREE DOG NIGHT"
ORIGINATED WITH THE ESKIMOS AND MEANS A
VERY COLD NIGHT, SO COLD THAT YOU HAVE TO
BED DOWN WITH THREE DOGS TO KEEP WARM.

THE AUSTRALIAN SEA WASP OR BOX JELLYFISH,
WHICH IS FOUND OFF THE COAST OF
QUEENSLAND, CAUSES DEATH WITHIN
3 MINUTES IF MEDICAL AID
ISN'T ADMINISTERED.

THE FASTEST BIRD IS THE SPINE-TAILED
SWIFT, CLOCKED AT SPEEDS OF UP TO
220 MPH (354 KM/H).

ARMADILLOS GET AN AVERAGE OF 18.5 HOURS
OF SLEEP PER DAY AND CAN WALK
UNDER WATER.

THE FASTEST MOVING LAND SNAIL, THE
COMMON GARDEN SNAIL, HAS A SPEED OF
0.0313 MPH (0.05 KM/H).

THE FIRST HOUSE RATS RECORDED IN
AMERICA APPEARED IN BOSTON IN 1775.

THE GIANT SQUID IS THE LARGEST CREATURE
WITHOUT A BACKBONE. IT WEIGHS UP TO 2.5
TONS AND GROWS UP TO 55 FT (16.7 M) LONG.
EACH EYE IS A FOOT (0.3 M) OR MORE
IN DIAMETER.

THE HARMLESS WHALE SHARK HOLDS THE
TITLE OF LARGEST FISH, WITH THE RECORD
BEING A 59 FOOTER (18 M) CAPTURED
IN THAILAND IN 1919.

ONE WAY TO TELL SEALS AND SEA LIONS APART
IS THAT SEA LIONS HAVE EXTERNAL EARS AND
TESTICLES.

THE HUMMINGBIRD IS THE ONLY BIRD THAT
CAN HOVER AND FLY STRAIGHT UP, DOWN,
OR BACKWARDS!

SOME CARNIVORES, RODENTS, BATS AND
INSECTIVORES HAVE A PENIS BONE,
CALLED A BACULUM.

A WHALE'S PENIS IS
CALLED A DORK.

THE KIWI, NATIONAL BIRD OF NEW ZEALAND, CAN'T FLY. IT LIVES IN A HOLE IN THE GROUND, IS ALMOST BLIND, AND LAYS ONLY ONE EGG EACH YEAR. DESPITE THIS, IT HAS SURVIVED FOR MORE THAN 70 MILLION YEARS.

CRICKETS HEAR THROUGH THEIR KNEES.

THE LARGEST ANIMAL EVER SEEN ALIVE WAS A 113.5 FT, (34 M) 170 TON FEMALE BLUE WHALE.

WHEN AN ARMADILLO IS FRIGHTENED
IT JUMPS STRAIGHT INTO THE AIR.

BIG BEN WAS SLOWED FIVE MINUTES ONE DAY
WHEN A PASSING GROUP OF STARLINGS
DECIDED TO TAKE A REST ON THE
MINUTE HAND OF THE CLOCK.

THE POLAR BEAR'S SKIN IS ACTUALLY BLACK.
THEIR HAIR IS HOLLOW AND ACTS LIKE
FIBEROPTICS, DIRECTING SUNLIGHT
TO WARM THEIR SKIN.

A PIG'S ORGASM LASTS FOR 30 MINUTES.

THE LARGEST BIRD EGG IN THE WORLD TODAY IS THAT OF THE OSTRICH. OSTRICH EGGS ARE FROM 6-8" (15-20 CM) LONG. BECAUSE OF THEIR SIZE AND THE THICKNESS OF THEIR SHELLS, THEY TAKE 40 MINUTES TO BOIL.

NEW ZEALAND KIWIS LAY THE LARGEST EGGS OF ANY BIRD, WITH RESPECT TO THEIR BODY SIZE.

THE LARGEST GREAT WHITE SHARK EVER
CAUGHT MEASURED 37 FT (11 M) AND WEIGHED
24,000 LBS (11,000 KG). IT WAS FOUND IN A
HERRING WEIR IN NEW BRUNSWICK IN 1930.

THE ONLY WAY TO STOP THE PAIN FROM THE
STING OF THE FLATHEAD FISH IS BY RUBBING
THE SLIME OF THE BELLY OF THE SAME FISH
THAT YOU WERE STUNG BY ON THE WOUND
THAT IT INFLICTED UPON YOU.

THE HUMMINGBIRD, THE LOON, THE SWIFT,
THE KINGFISHER, AND THE GREBE ARE
ALL BIRDS THAT CAN'T WALK.

THE LARGEST PIG ON RECORD WAS A POLAND-CHINA HOG NAMED BIG BILL, WHO WEIGHED 2,552 LBS (1158 KG).

WHEN A GIRAFFE'S BABY IS BORN IT FALLS FROM A HEIGHT OF 6 FT (1.8 M), NORMALLY WITHOUT BEING HURT.

THE LAST MEMBER OF THE FAMOUS BONAPARTE FAMILY, JEROME NAPOLEON BONAPARTE, DIED IN 1945, OF INJURIES SUSTAINED FROM TRIPPING OVER HIS DOG'S LEASH.

MANY SPECIES OF BIRD COPULATE IN THE AIR.
IN GENERAL, A COUPLE WILL FLY TO A VERY
HIGH ALTITUDE, AND THEN DROP. DURING
THEIR DESCENT, THE BIRDS MATE.

FROM ANCIENT TIMES IT WAS BELIEVED THAT
PORCUPINES COULD THROW THEIR QUILLS AT
AN ENEMY. THIS HAS LONG BEEN REFUTED,
AND EXPLAINED AS THE RESULT OF LOOSE
QUILLS BEING SHAKEN FREE.

THE MOUSE IS THE MOST COMMON
MAMMAL IN THE US.

A FLAMINGO CAN EAT ONLY WHEN
ITS HEAD IS UPSIDE DOWN.

ARMADILLOS HAVE FOUR BABIES AT A TIME,
ALWAYS ALL THE SAME SEX. THEY ARE PERFECT
QUADRUPLETS, THE FERTILIZED CELL SPLIT
INTO QUARTERS, RESULTING IN FOUR
IDENTICAL ARMADILLOS.

THE NAME OF THE DOG FROM "THE GRINCH
WHO STOLE CHRISTMAS" IS MAX.

IF NASA SENT BIRDS INTO SPACE THEY WOULD
SOON DIE OF STARVATION; THEY NEED
GRAVITY TO SWALLOW.

THE NAME OF THE DOG ON THE
CRACKER JACK BOX IS BINGO.

IT IS PHYSICALLY IMPOSSIBLE FOR
PIGS TO LOOK UP INTO THE SKY.

THE ONLY DOG TO EVER APPEAR IN A SHAKE-
SPEAREAN PLAY WAS "CRAB" IN "THE TWO
GENTLEMEN OF VERONA."

A PIG'S PENIS IS SHAPED LIKE
A CORKSCREW.

THE ONLY DOMESTIC ANIMAL NOT MENTIONED
IN THE BIBLE IS THE CAT.

A PENGUIN ONLY HAS SEX TWICE A YEAR.

THE PACIFIC GIANT OCTOPUS, THE LARGEST
OCTOPUS IN THE WORLD, GROWS FROM THE SIZE
OF A PEA TO A 150 LB (68 KG) BEHEMOTH
POTENTIALLY 30 FT (9 M) ACROSS IN ONLY
TWO YEARS; ITS ENTIRE LIFE SPAN.

SHRIMP CAN ONLY SWIM BACKWARDS.

THE PENALTY FOR KILLING A CAT, 4,000 YEARS AGO IN EGYPT, WAS DEATH.

SHRIMPS' HEARTS ARE IN THEIR HEADS.

THE PHRASE "RAINING CATS AND DOGS" ORIGINATED IN 17TH CENTURY ENGLAND. DURING HEAVY DOWNPOURS OF RAIN, MANY OF THESE POOR ANIMALS UNFORTUNATELY DROWNED AND THEIR BODIES WOULD BE SEEN FLOATING IN THE RAIN TORRENTS THAT RACED THROUGH THE STREETS. THE SITUATION GAVE THE APPEARANCE THAT IT HAD LITERALLY RAINED "CATS AND DOGS" AND LED TO THE CURRENT EXPRESSION.

STARFISH DON'T HAVE BRAINS.

THE PIGMY SHREW - A RELATIVE OF THE MOLE -
IS THE SMALLEST MAMMAL IN NORTH AMERICA.
IT WEIGHS 1/14 OUNCE - LESS THAN A DIME.

IF A FROG VOMITS, IT THROWS UP ITS STOMACH
FIRST, SO THE STOMACH IS DANGLING OUT OF
ITS MOUTH. THEN THE FROG USES ITS FORE-
ARMS TO DIG OUT ALL OF THE STOMACH'S
CONTENTS AND FINALLY SWALLOWS THE
STOMACH BACK DOWN AGAIN.

THE WORD RODENT COMES FROM THE LATIN
WORD RODERE MEANING TO GNAW.

THE POISONOUS COPPERHEAD SNAKE
SMELLS LIKE FRESH CUT CUCUMBERS.

A BABY EEL IS CALLED AN ELVER,
A BABY OYSTER IS CALLED A SPAT.

TIGERS HAVE STRIPED SKIN,
NOT JUST STRIPED FUR.

NOT ALL LEECHES FEED ON BLOOD. BUT IF YOU
NEED TO GET ONE OFF OF YOU, TRY USING YOUR
NAIL TO LOOSEN ITS JAWS AND THEN FLICK IT
OFF. (BY PULLING IT YOU MAY CAUSE FURTHER
DAMAGE TO THE WOUND, AND BY APPLYING
CHEMICALS, FIRE OR SOMETHING SIMILAR YOU
MAY CAUSE THE LEECH TO REGURGITATE ITS
STOMACH CONTENT, WHICH COULD CAUSE
INFECTION.) CLEAN WITH SOAP AND
WATER AFTERWARDS!

ELEPHANTS HAVE BEEN FOUND SWIMMING
MILES FROM SHORE IN THE INDIAN OCEAN.

THE SMITHSONIAN NATIONAL MUSEUM OF NATURAL HISTORY HOUSES THE WORLD'S LARGEST SHELL COLLECTION, SOME 15 MILLION SPECIMENS.

THE LONGEST RECORDED FLIGHT OF A CHICKEN IS 13 SECONDS.

THE TERM "DOG DAYS" HAS NOTHING TO DO WITH DOGS. IT DATES BACK TO ROMAN TIMES, WHEN IT WAS BELIEVED THAT SIRIUS, THE DOG STAR, ADDED ITS HEAT TO THAT OF THE SUN FROM JULY 3 - AUGUST 11, CREATING EXCEPTIONALLY HIGH TEMPERATURES. THE ROMANS CALLED THE PERIOD DIES CANICULARES, OR "DAYS OF THE DOG."

THE TURBOT FISH LAYS APPROXIMATELY
14 MILLION EGGS DURING ITS LIFETIME.

THE TURKEY WAS NAMED FOR WHAT WAS
WRONGLY THOUGHT TO BE ITS
COUNTRY OF ORIGIN.

THE UNDERSIDE OF A HORSE'S HOOF IS CALLED
A FROG. THE FROG PEELS OFF SEVERAL
TIMES A YEAR WITH NEW GROWTH.

EMUS CAN'T WALK BACKWARDS.

NINETY-NINE PERCENT OF ALL LOBSTERS DIE
A FEW WEEKS AFTER HATCHING. IN FACT, THE
ODDS ARE 10,000 TO 1 AGAINST ANY LARVAL
LOBSTER LIVING LONG ENOUGH TO END
UP AS A LOBSTER DINNER.

A DOLPHIN'S HEARING IS SO ACUTE THAT IT
CAN PICK UP AN UNDERWATER SOUND
FROM 15 MILES (24 KM) AWAY.

THE POISON-ARROW FROG HAS ENOUGH
POISON TO KILL ABOUT 2,200 PEOPLE.

THE VISCERA OF JAPANESE ABALONE CAN
HARBOUR A POISONOUS SUBSTANCE, WHICH
CAUSES A BURNING, STINGING, PRICKLING AND
ITCHING OVER THE ENTIRE BODY. IT DOESN'T
MANIFEST ITSELF UNTIL EXPOSURE TO
SUNLIGHT - IF EATEN OUTDOORS IN SUNLIGHT,
SYMPTOMS OCCUR QUICKLY AND SUDDENLY.

THE WORLD RECORD FROG JUMP IS 33 FT, 5.5 IN (15 M, 14 CM) OVER THE COURSE OF 3 CONSECUTIVE LEAPS, ACHIEVED IN MAY 1977 BY A SOUTH AFRICAN SHARP -NOSED FROG CALLED SANTJIE.

THE WORLD'S LARGEST MAMMAL, THE BLUE WHALE, WEIGHS 50 TONS AT BIRTH. FULLY GROWN, IT WEIGHS AS MUCH AS 150 TONS.

STAG BEETLES HAVE STRONGER MANDIBLES THAN HUMANS.

"EAT LIKE A BIRD?"
MANY BIRDS EAT TWICE THEIR WEIGHT A DAY.

BEES MUST COLLECT THE NECTAR FROM TWO
THOUSAND FLOWERS TO MAKE ONE TABLE-
SPOONFUL OF HONEY.

THE WORLD'S LARGEST RODENT IS THE
CAPYBARA, AN AMAZON WATER HOG THAT LOOKS
LIKE A GUINEA PIG. IT CAN WEIGH MORE THAN
100 LBS (45 KG).

THE WORLD'S SMALLEST MAMMAL IS
THE BUMBLEBEE BAT OF THAILAND,
WEIGHING LESS THAN A PENNY.

THERE ARE AROUND 2,600 DIFFERENT SPECIES
OF FROGS. THEY LIVE ON EVERY CONTINENT
EXCEPT ANTARCTICA.

A FULL-GROWN BEAR CAN RUN AS FAST
AS A HORSE.

THERE ARE MORE THAN 100 MILLION DOGS AND CATS IN THE UNITED STATES. AMERICANS SPEND MORE THAN 5.4 BILLION DOLLARS ON THEIR PETS EACH YEAR.

THERE IS NO SINGLE CAT CALLED THE PANTHER. THE NAME IS COMMONLY APPLIED TO THE LEOPARD, BUT IT IS ALSO USED TO REFER TO THE PUMA AND THE JAGUAR. A BLACK PANTHER IS REALLY A BLACK LEOPARD.

IT IS POSSIBLE TO LEAD A COW UPSTAIRS BUT NOT DOWNSTAIRS, BECAUSE A COW'S KNEES CAN'T BEND PROPERLY TO WALK BACK DOWN.

TURKEYS ORIGINATED IN NORTH AND CENTRAL AMERICA, AND EVIDENCE INDICATES THAT THEY HAVE BEEN AROUND FOR OVER 10 MILLION YEARS.

RHINOS ARE IN THE SAME FAMILY AS HORSES, AND ARE THOUGHT TO HAVE INSPIRED THE MYTH OF THE UNICORN.

UNLIKE MOST FISH, ELECTRIC EELS CAN'T GET ENOUGH OXYGEN FROM WATER. APPROXIMATELY EVERY FIVE MINUTES, THEY MUST SURFACE TO BREATHE, OR THEY WILL DROWN. UNLIKE MOST FISH, THEY CAN SWIM BOTH BACKWARDS AND FORWARDS.

BRAZORIA COUNTY IN SOUTHEAST TEXAS IS THE ONLY COUNTY IN THE UNITED STATES AND CANADA TO HAVE EVERY KIND OF POISONOUS SNAKE FOUND IN THOSE TWO COUNTRIES.

WHALES AND DOLPHINS CAN LITERALLY FALL HALF ASLEEP. THEIR BRAIN HEMISPHERES ALTERNATE SLEEPING, SO THE ANIMALS CAN CONTINUE TO SURFACE AND BREATHE.

WHEN A FEMALE HORSE AND MALE DONKEY MATE, THE OFFSPRING IS CALLED A MULE, BUT WHEN A MALE HORSE AND FEMALE DONKEY MATE, THE OFFSPRING IS CALLED A HINNY.

A DUCK'S QUACK DOESN'T ECHO,
AND NO ONE KNOWS WHY.

WHEN THE BLACK DEATH SWEPT ACROSS
ENGLAND, ONE THEORY WAS THAT CATS CAUSED
THE PLAGUE. THOUSANDS WERE SLAUGHTERED.
IRONICALLY, THOSE THAT KEPT THEIR CATS
WERE LESS AFFECTED, BECAUSE THEY KEPT
THEIR HOUSES CLEAR OF THE REAL
CULPRITS: RATS.

A GROUP OF GEESE ON THE GROUND
IS A GAGGLE;
A GROUP OF GEESE IN THE AIR IS A SKEIN.

WORLDWIDE, GOATS PROVIDE PEOPLE WITH
MORE MEAT AND MILK THAN ANY
OTHER DOMESTIC ANIMAL.

THE ONLY CONTINENT WITHOUT REPTILES
OR SNAKES IS ANTARCTICA.

ROOSTERS CAN'T CROW IF THEY CAN'T
FULLY EXTEND THEIR NECKS.

A COCKROACH CAN LIVE
UP TO A WEEK WITHOUT A HEAD.

THE FINGERPRINTS OF KOALAS ARE VIRTUALLY
INDISTINGUISHABLE FROM THOSE OF HUMANS,
SO MUCH SO THAT THEY COULD BE CONFUSED
AT A CRIME SCENE.

A TYPICAL BED USUALLY HOUSES
OVER 6 BILLION DUST MITES.

EMUS HAVE DOUBLE-PLUMED FEATHERS,
AND THEY LAY EMERALD/FOREST GREEN EGGS.

AMAZON ANTS (RED ANTS FOUND IN THE
WESTERN U.S.) STEAL THE LARVA OF OTHER
ANTS TO KEEP AS SLAVES. THE SLAVE ANTS
BUILD HOMES FOR AND FEED THE AMAZON ANTS,
WHO CAN'T DO ANYTHING BUT FIGHT.
THEY DEPEND COMPLETELY ON THEIR
SLAVES FOR SURVIVAL.

THE COMMON GOLDFISH IS THE ONLY ANIMAL
THAT CAN SEE BOTH INFRARED
AND ULTRAVIOLET LIGHT.

AN ADULT BEDBUG CAN SURVIVE UP TO
ONE YEAR WITHOUT FEEDING.

YOUNG CATS CAN DISTINGUISH BETWEEN TWO
IDENTICAL SOUNDS THAT ARE JUST 18" APART
AT A DISTANCE OF UP TO 60 FT (8 M).

AN INFESTATION OF HEAD LICE
IS CALLED PEDICULOSIS.

YOU CHECK YOUR CATS PULSE ON THE INSIDE OF
THE BACK THIGH, WHERE THE LEG JOINS TO THE
BODY. NORMAL FOR CATS: 110-170 BEATS
PER MINUTE.

ANTS ARE SOCIAL INSECTS AND LIVE IN
COLONIES, WHICH MAY HAVE AS MANY AS
500,000 INDIVIDUALS.

YOU CAN TELL A CAT'S MOOD BY LOOKING INTO
ITS EYES. A FRIGHTENED OR EXCITED CAT WILL
HAVE LARGE, ROUND PUPILS. AN ANGRY CAT
WILL HAVE NARROW PUPILS. THE PUPIL SIZE IS
RELATED AS MUCH TO THE CAT'S EMOTIONS
AS TO THE DEGREE OF LIGHT.

ANTS DON'T SLEEP.

WINSTON CHURCHILL ADORED CATS.
CHURCHILL USED TO REFER TO HIS CAT, JOCK,
AS HIS SPECIAL ASSISTANT. JOCK WAS REPORT-
ED TO BE ON THE BED WITH HIS MASTER ON THE
DAY THE GREAT BRITISH STATESMAN DIED.

APHIDS ARE BORN PREGNANT WITHOUT THE
BENEFIT OF SEX. APHIDS CAN GIVE BIRTH 10
DAYS AFTER BEING BORN THEMSELVES.

WHEN YOUR CAT RUBS UP AGAINST YOU, SHE IS ACTUALLY MARKING YOU AS "HERS" WITH HER SCENT. IF YOUR CAT PUSHES HER FACE AGAINST YOUR HEAD, IT IS A SIGN OF ACCEPTANCE AND AFFECTION.

WHEN YOU FIND YOUR CAT GLUED TO THE WINDOW INTENTLY WATCHING A BIRD, MAKING A STRANGE CHATTERING NOISE AND CLICKING HIS OR HER JAWS ODDLY, YOUR CAT IS MERELY ACTING ON INSTINCT. WHAT YOUR CAT IS DOING IS DIRECTLY RELATED TO THE KILLING BITE THAT ALL CATS (BOTH DOMESTIC AND WILD CATS) USE TO DISPATCH THEIR PREY.

DRAGONFLIES ARE ONE OF THE FASTEST IN-
SECTS, FLYING 50-60 MPH (80-100 KM/H).

TO DRINK, A CAT LAPS LIQUID FROM THE
UNDERSIDE OF ITS TONGUE, RATHER
THAN THE TOP.

EACH YEAR, INSECTS EAT 1/3
OF THE EARTH'S FOOD CROP.

HUMANS BEGAN TO DOMESTICATE HORSES
AROUND 4000 BC.

THE TURKISH VAN, A VERY OLD RARE CAT BREED
THAT ORIGINATED IN TURKEY, IS QUITE
DIFFERENT FROM OTHER BREEDS BECAUSE OF
ITS UNUSUAL LOVE OF WATER. KNOWN AS
"THE SWIMMING CAT," THE VAN IS
STRONG, QUICK AND AGILE.

MOSQUITOES DISLIKE CITRONELLA
BECAUSE IT IRRITATES THEIR FEET.

THE PHENOMENON OF CATS FINDING THEIR
OWNERS IN A PLACE WHERE THEY HAVE NEVER
BEEN BEFORE IS SCIENTIFICALLY KNOWN AS
PSI-TRAILING. MANY WELL-DOCUMENTED
STORIES TELL OF CATS THAT HAVE WALKED
HUNDREDS, EVEN THOUSANDS OF
MILES/KILOMETERS TO FIND
THEIR OWNERS.

MOSQUITOES PREFER CHILDREN TO ADULTS,
AND BLONDES TO BRUNETTES.

THE PERSIAN CAT HAS THE LONGEST AND
THICKEST FUR OF ALL DOMESTIC CATS.
THE TOPCOAT MAY BE UP TO 5" LONG.

NO TWO SPIDER WEBS ARE THE SAME.

THE MORE CATS ARE SPOKEN TO,
THE MORE THEY WILL SPEAK BACK.

ONLY FEMALE MOSQUITOES BITE. FEMALES
NEED THE PROTEIN FROM BLOOD
TO PRODUCE THEIR EGGS.

THE MAINE COON IS 4-5 TIMES LARGER THAN
THE SINGAPURA, THE SMALLEST BREED OF CAT.
THE MAINE COON IS THE ONLY NATIVE
AMERICAN LONGHAIRED BREED.

ONLY FULL-GROWN MALE CRICKETS CAN CHIRP.

THE HEAVIEST CAT EVER RECORDED
WEIGHED 46 LBS (21 KG).

HORSES HAVE A SKELETON THAT
AVERAGES 205 BONES.

THE FIRST CAT SHOW WAS HELD IN 1871 AT
THE CRYSTAL PALACE IN LONDON.

THE BLOOD OF MAMMALS IS RED,
THE BLOOD OF INSECTS IS YELLOW,
AND THE BLOOD OF LOBSTERS IS BLUE.

THE DIFFERENT TYPES OF TABBY PATTERNS
THAT ARE SEEN IN DOMESTIC CATS ALSO
OCCUR IN WILD CATS.

THE BUZZ THAT YOU HEAR WHEN A BEE
APPROACHES IS THE SOUND OF ITS FOUR WINGS
MOVING AT 11,400 STROKES PER MINUTE.
BEES FLY AN AVERAGE OF 15 MPH (24 KM/H).

HORSE-DONKEY HYBRIDS (MULES AND HINNIES)
ARE ALMOST ALWAYS STERILE BECAUSE HORSES
HAVE 64 CHROMOSOMES WHEREAS DONKEYS
HAVE 62, PRODUCING OFFSPRING WITH 63
CHROMOSOMES.

THE DISEASE-CARRYING MOSQUITO,
DELIVERING ENCEPHALITIS, THE WEST NILE
VIRUS, MALARIA, AND DENGUE FEVER, IS BY FAR
THE DEADLIEST BEAST IN THE ANIMAL WORLD.
THE WORLD HEALTH ORGANIZATION SAYS
MOSQUITOES CAUSE MORE THAN 2 MILLION
DEATHS A YEAR WORLDWIDE.

THE HONEYBEE KILLS MORE PEOPLE
WORLDWIDE THAN ALL THE
POISONOUS SNAKES COMBINED.

THE CAT'S FOOTPADS ABSORB THE SHOCKS
OF THE LANDING WHEN THE CAT JUMPS.

THE LARGEST COCKROACH ON RECORD IS
ONE MEASURED AT 3.81" IN LENGTH.

THE CATNIP PLANT CONTAINS OIL CALLED
HEPETALACTONE, WHICH DOES FOR CATS WHAT
MARIJUANA DOES TO SOME PEOPLE. NOT ALL
CATS REACT TO IT, BUT THOSE THAT DO APPEAR
TO ENTER A TRANCELIKE STATE.
A POSITIVE REACTION TAKES THE FORM OF THE
CAT SNIFFING THE CATNIP, THEN LICKING,
BITING, CHEWING IT, RUBBING AND ROLLING ON
IT REPEATEDLY, PURRING, MEOWING AND EVEN
LEAPING INTO THE AIR.

THE LARGEST INSECT EGG BELONGS TO THE
MALAYSIAN JUNGLE NYMPH, A STICKLIKE
INSECT THAT MEASURES ABOUT 0.5" (1.3 CM)
LONG, THAT LAY EGGS LARGER THAN A PEANUT!
(SOME INSECTS, MAINLY MANTISES AND
COCKROACHES, LAY EGG CASES THAT
ARE LARGER, BUT THEY CONTAIN ABOUT
200 INDIVIDUAL EGGS.)

THE CATGUT FORMERLY USED AS STRINGS IN
TENNIS RACKETS AND MUSICAL INSTRUMENTS
DOESN'T COME FROM CATS. CATGUT ACTUALLY
COMES FROM SHEEP, HOGS, AND HORSES.

THE LEAP OF AN AVERAGE FLEA IS EQUIVALENT
TO A 100 POUND (45,5 KG) HUMAN LEAPING
1,000 MI (1609 KM) AND ENDURING A G-FORCE
OF 20,000 LBS (9072 KG) WITH ACCELERATION
GREATER THAN THAT OF A SPACE SHUTTLE.

THE CAT WAS DOMESTICATED OVER 4,000 YEARS AGO. TODAY'S HOUSE CATS ARE DESCENDED FROM WILDCATS IN AFRICA AND EUROPE.

THE TSETSE FLY KILLS
66,000 PEOPLE ANNUALLY.

THE CAT HAS 500 SKELETAL MUSCLES
(HUMANS HAVE 650).

THE VENOM OF A FEMALE BLACK WIDOW
SPIDER IS MORE POTENT THAN THAT
OF A RATTLESNAKE.

THE CAT FAMILY SPLIT FROM THE OTHER
MAMMALS AT LEAST 40 MILLION YEARS AGO,
MAKING THEM ONE OF THE OLDEST
MAMMALIAN FAMILIES.

THE WORLD'S SMALLEST WINGED INSECT,
THE TANZANIAN PARASITIC WASP, IS SMALLER
THAN THE EYE OF A HOUSEFLY.

THE AVERAGE CANNED OR DRY CAT MEAL
IS THE NUTRITIONAL EQUIVALENT OF
EATING FIVE MICE.

THERE ARE MORE INSECTS IN ONE SQUARE
MILE OF RURAL LAND THAN THERE ARE
HUMAN BEINGS ON THE ENTIRE EARTH.

THE ANCIENT EGYPTIAN WORD FOR
CAT WAS MAU, WHICH MEANS "TO SEE."

THERE ARE MORE THAN 2,500
VARIETIES OF MOSQUITO.

THE ANCESTOR OF ALL DOMESTIC CATS
IS THE AFRICAN WILD CAT, WHICH
STILL EXISTS TODAY.

THERE ARE MORE THAN 900,000 KNOWN
SPECIES OF INSECTS IN THE WORLD.

WHEN A QUEEN BEE LAYS THE FERTILIZED EGGS THAT WILL DEVELOP INTO NEW QUEENS, ONLY ONE OF THE NEWLY LAID QUEENS ACTUALLY SURVIVES. THE FIRST NEW QUEEN THAT EMERGES FROM HER CELL DESTROYS ALL OTHER QUEENS IN THEIR CELLS AND, THEREAFTER, REIGNS ALONE.

SOME COMMON HOUSEPLANTS POISONOUS TO CATS INCLUDE: ENGLISH IVY, IRIS, MISTLETOE AND PHILODENDRON.

WHEN ANTS FIND FOOD, THEY LAY DOWN A CHEMICAL TRAIL, CALLED A PHEROMONE, SO THAT OTHER ANTS CAN FIND THEIR WAY FROM THE NEST TO THE FOOD SOURCE.

SIR ISAAC NEWTON, WHO FIRST DESCRIBED
THE PRINCIPLE OF GRAVITY, ALSO INVENTED
THE CAT FLAP FOR THE CONVENIENCE OF
HIS MANY CATS.

WORKER ANTS MAY LIVE SEVEN YEARS AND
THE QUEEN MAY LIVE AS LONG AS 15 YEARS.

SIAMESE KITTENS ARE BORN WHITE BECAUSE
OF THE HEAT INSIDE THE MOTHER'S UTERUS
BEFORE BIRTH. THIS HEAT KEEPS THE KITTENS'
HAIR FROM DARKENING ON THE POINTS.

YOU'RE MORE LIKELY TO BE A TARGET
FOR MOSQUITOES IF YOU CONSUME BANANAS.

SIAMESE CATS ORIGINATED IN SIAM – MODERN
DAY THAILAND. LEGEND HAS IT THAT THEY
WERE THE COMPANIONS OF KINGS AND PRIESTS
AND THAT THEY GUARDED TEMPLES. SOME
TRACE SIAMESE ORIGINS TO EGYPT AND BURMA,
BUT MANY DISPUTE THIS. SIAMESE WERE FIRST
BROUGHT TO ENGLAND IN THE LATE 1800S.

A DOG'S WHISKERS ARE TOUCH-SENSITIVE HAIRS CALLED VIBRISSAE. THEY ARE FOUND ON THE MUZZLE, ABOVE THE EYES AND BELOW THE JAWS, AND CAN ACTUALLY SENSE TINY CHANGES IN AIRFLOW.

RETRACTABLE CLAWS ARE A PHYSICAL PHENOMENON THAT SETS CATS APART FROM THE REST OF THE ANIMAL KINGDOM.

ACCORDING TO A RECENT SURVEY, THE MOST POPULAR NAME FOR A DOG IS MAX. OTHER POPULAR NAMES INCLUDE MOLLY, SAM, ZACH, AND MAGGIE.

PURRING IS PART OF EVERY CAT'S REPERTOIRE OF SOCIAL COMMUNICATION, APPARENTLY CREATED BY THE MOVEMENT OF AIR THROUGH CONTRACTIONS OF THE DIAPHRAGM. INTERESTINGLY, PURRING IS SOMETIMES HEARD IN CATS THAT ARE SEVERELY ILL OR ANXIOUS, PERHAPS AS A SELF-COMFORTING VOCALIZATION. BUT, MORE TYPICALLY, IT IS A SIGN OF CONTENTMENT, FIRST HEARD IN KITTENS AS THEY SUCKLE MILK FROM THEIR MOTHER.

ACCORDING TO ANCIENT GREEK LITERATURE, WHEN ODYSSEUS ARRIVED HOME AFTER AN ABSENCE OF 20 YEARS, DISGUISED AS A BEGGAR, THE ONLY ONE TO RECOGNIZE HIM WAS HIS AGED DOG ARGOS, WHO WAGGED HIS TAIL AT HIS MASTER, AND THEN DIED.

ONE OF THE OLDEST KNOWN FEMALE CATS WAS
MA, FROM DEVON, WHO WAS 34 WHEN
SHE DIED IN 1957.

AN AMERICAN ANIMAL HOSPITAL ASSOCIATION
POLL SHOWED THAT 33% OF DOG OWNERS ADMIT
THAT THEY TALK TO THEIR DOGS ON THE PHONE
OR LEAVE MESSAGES ON THE ANSWERING
MACHINE WHILE AWAY.

AN ESTIMATED 1 MILLION DOGS IN THE UNITED
STATES HAVE BEEN NAMED THE PRIMARY
BENEFICIARY IN THEIR OWNER'S WILL.

ORANGE AND LEMON RINDS ARE OFFENSIVE TO CATS. A LIGHT RUBBING OF ORANGE PEEL ON FURNITURE WILL DISCOURAGE YOUR CAT FROM USING IT AS A SCRATCHING POST.

BARBARA BUSH'S BOOK ABOUT HER ENGLISH SPRINGER SPANIEL, MILLIE'S BOOK, WAS ON THE BESTSELLER LIST FOR 29 WEEKS. MILLIE WAS THE MOST POPULAR "FIRST DOG" IN HISTORY.

ONE LITTER BOX PER CAT, PLUS AN EXTRA BOX, IS THE BEST FORMULA FOR A MULTI-CAT HOUSEHOLD.

BEFORE THE ENACTMENT OF THE 1978 LAW THAT MADE IT MANDATORY FOR DOG OWNERS IN NEW YORK CITY TO CLEAN UP AFTER THEIR PETS, APPROXIMATELY 40 MILLION LBS (18 MILLION KG) OF DOG EXCREMENT WERE DEPOSITED ON THE STREETS EVERY YEAR.

IN MOST CLAMS, TWO ADDUCTOR MUSCLES CONTRACT TO CLOSE THE SHELLS. THE CLAM HAS NO HEAD, AND USUALLY NO EYES.

THE GIANT CLAM IS PLANKTONIC AS A LARVA, BUT BECOME SESSILE (NOT ABLE TO MOVE AROUND) IN ADULTHOOD.

OF ALL THE SPECIES OF CATS, THE DOMESTIC
CAT IS THE ONLY SPECIES ABLE TO HOLD ITS
TAIL VERTICALLY WHILE WALKING. ALL SPECIES
OF WILD CATS HOLD THEIR TALK HORIZONTALLY
OR TUCKED BETWEEN THEIR LEGS
WHILE WALKING.

CATS HAVE A BETTER MEMORY THAN DOGS.
TESTS CONDUCTED BY THE UNIVERSITY OF
MICHIGAN CONCLUDED THAT WHILE A DOG'S
MEMORY LASTS NO MORE THAN 5 MINUTES, A
CAT'S COULD LAST AS LONG AS 16 HOURS – THAT
MEANS THAT CAT'S MEMORY EXCEEDS EVEN
MONKEYS AND ORANGUTANS!

MOLLUSCS HAVE SUCH A VARIED RANGE OF
BODY STRUCTURES THAT IT IS DIFFICULT TO
FIND DEFINING CHARACTERISTICS THAT
APPLY TO ALL MODERN GROUPS.

NOT EVERY CAT GETS "HIGH" FROM CATNIP.
WHETHER OR NOT A CAT RESPONDS TO IT
DEPENDS UPON A RECESSIVE GENE:
NO GENE, NO JOY.

KLEPTOPARASITISM IS A FORM OF FEEDING
WHERE ONE ANIMAL TAKES PREY FROM
ANOTHER THAT HAS CAUGHT, KILLED,
OR OTHERWISE PREPARED THE PREY,
INCLUDING STORED FOOD.

CATS HAVE MORE THAN ONE HUNDRED VOCAL SOUNDS, WHILE DOGS ONLY HAVE ABOUT TEN.

THE DISTINCTIVE BUZZ OF A FLYING BUMBLEBEE HAS INSPIRED THE ORCHESTRAL INTERLUDE "FLIGHT OF THE BUMBLEBEE."

NOSTRADAMUS, THE FRENCH ASTROLOGER, 1503-1566, HAD A CAT NAMED GRIMALKIN. GRIMALKIN WAS ALSO THE NAME OF A FAIRY CAT FROM THE HIGHLANDS IN A SCOTTISH LEGEND.

THE GIANT PANDA'S LATIN NAME, AILUROPODA MELANOLEUCA, LITERALLY MEANS, "CAT-FOOT BLACK-AND-WHITE."

CATS, NOT DOGS, ARE THE MOST COMMON PETS IN AMERICA. THERE ARE APPROXIMATELY 66 MILLION CATS TO 58 MILLION DOGS, WITH PARAKEETS A DISTANT THIRD AT 14 MILLION.

IN MANY PLACES AROUND THE WORLD, GRASSHOPPERS ARE EATEN AS A GOOD SOURCE OF PROTEIN.

NEWBORN KITTENS HAVE CLOSED EAR CANALS THAT DON'T BEGIN TO OPEN FOR 9 DAYS.

IN INDIA, GREEN IGUANAS ARE CAPTURED FOR THEIR MEAT. THE TAIL IS CONSIDERED A DELICACY AND THE FAT OF THE BODY IS BOILED DOWN. THE RESULTING OIL IS, FOR EXAMPLE, USED AS A CURE FOR IMPOTENCE.

CONTRARY TO POPULAR BELIEF, DOGS DO NOT SWEAT BY SALIVATING. THEY SWEAT THROUGH THE PADS OF THEIR FEET.

THERE ARE NUMEROUS ISLANDS FROM WHICH
SNAKES ARE CONSPICUOUSLY ABSENT SUCH AS
IRELAND, ICELAND AND NEW ZEALAND.

NEVER PICK A KITTEN UP BY THE NECK.
ONLY A MOTHER CAT MAY DO THIS SAFELY.

TAPIRS ARE GENERALLY SHY, BUT WHEN THEY
ARE SCARED THEY CAN DEFEND THEMSELVES
WITH THEIR VERY POWERFUL JAWS. IN 1998, A
ZOOKEEPER IN OKLAHOMA CITY WAS MAULED
AND HAD AN ARM SEVERED BY A TAPIR BITE,
AFTER SHE ATTEMPTED TO FEED THE
ATTACKING TAPIR'S YOUNG.

DACHSHUNDS ARE THE SMALLEST BREEDS OF
DOG USED FOR HUNTING. THEY ARE LOW TO THE
GROUND, WHICH ALLOWS THEM TO ENTER AND
MANEUVER THROUGH TUNNELS EASILY.

KOALAS RARELY DRINK WATER, DUE TO THEIR
DIET OF EUCALYPTUS LEAVES. EUCALYPTUS
LEAVES CONTAIN ENOUGH MOISTURE TO SUPPLY
MOST OF THE KOALA'S WATER NEEDS.

NEUTERING A CAT EXTENDS ITS LIFE
SPAN BY TWO OR THREE YEARS.

KOALAS ARE NOT RELATED TO BEARS.

SQUIDS HAVE THREE HEARTS.

A HIPPOPOTAMUS CAN STAY UNDER WATER
FOR UP TO 30 MINUTES.

MOTHER CATS TEACH THEIR KITTENS
TO USE THE LITTER BOX.

THE BLACK BULLDOG ANT FROM AUSTRALIA IS
THE MOST DANGEROUS ANT IN THE WORLD.
IT STINGS AND BITES AT THE SAME TIME
AND HAS BEEN KNOWN TO KILL HUMANS.

DOGS ARE MENTIONED 14 TIMES IN THE BIBLE.

MANY SNAKES NEVER STOP GROWING.
THAT'S ONE REASON WHY THEY MUST
SHED THEIR SKIN.

MOST CATS HAVE NO EYELASHES.

THE SLOWEST MAMMAL ON EARTH IS THE
TREE SLOTH. IT MOVES AT A SPEED
OF 6 FT (1.8 M) PER MINUTE.

DOGS CAN HEAR SOUNDS THAT ARE TOO FAINT FOR US TO HEAR, AND CAN ALSO HEAR NOISES AT A MUCH HIGHER FREQUENCY THAN WE CAN. THEIR HEARING IS SO GOOD THAT THEY PROBABLY RELY MORE ON SOUND THAN ON SIGHT TO NAVIGATE THEIR WORLD.

MORRIS, THE 9 LIVES CAT, WAS DISCOVERED AT AN ANIMAL SHELTER IN NEW ENGLAND.

THE STRONGEST ANIMAL IN THE WORLD IS THE RHINOCEROS BEETLE. IT CAN LIFT 850 TIMES ITS OWN WEIGHT.

DOGS' EYES HAVE LARGE PUPILS AND A WIDE FIELD OF VISION, MAKING THEM REALLY GOOD AT FOLLOWING MOVING OBJECTS.
DOGS ALSO SEE WELL IN FAIRLY LOW LIGHT.

KATYDIDS HAVE EARS IN THEIR FRONT LEGS.

MANY PEOPLE FEAR CATCHING A PROTOZOAN DISEASE, TOXOPLASMOSIS, FROM CATS. THIS DISEASE CAN CAUSE ILLNESS IN A HUMAN, BUT MORE SERIOUSLY, CAN CAUSE BIRTH DEFECTS IN THE UNBORN. TOXOPLASMOSIS IS A COMMON DISEASE, SOMETIMES SPREAD THROUGH THE FAECES OF CATS. IT IS CAUSED MOST OFTEN FROM EATING RAW OR RARE BEEF. PREGNANT WOMEN AND PEOPLE WITH A DEPRESSED IMMUNE SYSTEM SHOULD NOT TOUCH THE CAT LITTER BOX. OTHER THAN THAT, THERE IS NO REASON THAT THESE PEOPLE HAVE TO AVOID CATS.

DOGS HAVE FAR FEWER TASTE BUDS THAN
PEOPLE – PROBABLY FEWER THAN 2,000. IT
IS THE SMELL THAT INITIALLY ATTRACTS
THEM TO A PARTICULAR FOOD.

MANY OF A CAT'S BONES ARE FOUND IN ITS TAIL.

ALL POLAR BEARS ARE LEFT-HANDED.

DOGS IN MONUMENTS: THE DOG IS PLACED AT
THE FEET OF WOMEN IN MONUMENTS TO
SYMBOLISE AFFECTION AND FIDELITY, AS A
LION IS PLACED AT THE FEET OF MEN TO SIGNIFY
COURAGE AND MAGNANIMITY.
MANY OF THE CRUSADERS ARE REPRESENTED
WITH THEIR FOOT ON A DOG, TO SHOW THAT
THEY FOLLOWED THE STANDARD OF THE LORD
AS FAITHFULLY AS A DOG FOLLOWS
THE FOOTSTEPS OF HIS MASTER.

AFTER EATING, A HOUSEFLY REGURGITATES
ITS FOOD AND THEN EATS IT AGAIN.

MANY CATS ARE UNABLE TO PROPERLY DIGEST COW'S MILK. MILK AND MILK PRODUCTS GIVE THEM DIARRHEA.

A HIPPO CAN OPEN ITS MOUTH WIDE ENOUGH TO FIT A 4 FT (1.2 M) TALL CHILD INSIDE.

DOGS MAY NOT HAVE AS MANY TASTE BUDS AS WE DO (THEY HAVE ABOUT 2,000 ON THEIR TONGUES, WHILE WE HUMANS HAVE ABOUT 9,000), BUT THAT DOESN'T MEAN THEY'RE NOT DISCRIMINATING EATERS. THEY HAVE OVER 200 MILLION SCENT RECEPTORS IN THEIR NOSES (WE HAVE ONLY 5 MILLION) SO IT'S IMPORTANT THAT THEIR FOOD SMELLS AND TASTES GOOD.

A HEDGEHOG'S HEART BEATS 300
TIMES A MINUTE ON AVERAGE.

LUCY WEBB HAYES, WIFE OF RUTHERFORD
HAYES, IS THE FIRST PERSON RECORDED TO
OWN A SIAMESE IN THE U.S.

A CROCODILE GROWS NEW TEETH THROUGHOUT
ITS ENTIRE LIFE TO REPLACE OLD TEETH.

EACH DAY IN THE US, ANIMAL SHELTERS PUT
30,000 HOMELESS DOGS AND CATS TO SLEEP.

RATS MULTIPLY SO QUICKLY THAT IN
18 MONTHS, TWO RATS COULD HAVE
OVER 1 MILLION DESCENDANTS.

IN A STUDY OF 200,000 OSTRICHES OVER
A PERIOD OF 80 YEARS, NO ONE REPORTED
A SINGLE CASE WHERE AN OSTRICH
BURIED ITS HEAD IN THE SAND.

BABOONS CAN RAID HUMAN DWELLINGS AND IN
SOUTH AFRICA THEY HAVE BEEN KNOWN
TO PREY ON SHEEP AND GOATS.

THE AVERAGE CHOCOLATE BAR HAS
8 INSECTS' LEGS IN IT.

KITTENS REMAIN WITH THEIR MOTHER
TILL THE AGE OF 9 WEEKS.

TO ESCAPE THE GRIP OF A CROCODILE'S JAWS, PUSH YOUR THUMBS INTO ITS EYEBALLS AND IT WILL LET YOU GO INSTANTLY.

FOR STEPHEN KING'S "CUJO" (1983), FIVE ST. BERNARDS', ONE MECHANICAL HEAD, AND AN ACTOR IN A DOG COSTUME WERE USED TO PLAY THE TITLE CHARACTER.

ELEPHANTS' TRUNKS CAN BE UP TO 7 FT (2.1 M) LONG AND WEIGH UP TO 300 LBS (1360 KG).

JAGUARS ARE THE ONLY BIG CATS
THAT DON'T ROAR.

FRENCH POODLES DID NOT ORIGINATE IN
FRANCE. POODLES WERE ORIGINALLY USED AS
HUNTING DOGS IN EUROPE. THE DOGS' THICK
COATS WERE A HINDRANCE IN WATER AND THICK
BRUSH, SO HUNTERS SHEARED THE HINDQUAR-
TERS, WITH CUFFS LEFT AROUND THE ANKLES
AND HIPS TO PROTECT AGAINST RHEUMATISM.
EACH HUNTER MARKED HIS DOGS' HEADS
WITH A RIBBON OF HIS OWN COLOR,
ALLOWING GROUPS OF HUNTERS TO
TELL THEIR DOGS APART.

LIZARDS COMMUNICATE
BY DOING PUSH-UPS.

IT HAS BEEN SCIENTIFICALLY PROVEN THAT
STROKING A CAT CAN LOWER ONE'S
BLOOD PRESSURE.

FISH CAN DROWN.

AFRICAN ELEPHANTS TAKE AT LEAST
3 BATHS A DAY.

INBREEDING CAUSES 3 OUT OF EVERY 10
DALMATIAN DOGS TO SUFFER FROM
HEARING DISABILITY.

MALE SATIN BOWERBIRDS BUILD "BOWERS" OR
SHELTERS, OUT OF STICKS AND LEAVES. THE
BIRDS DECORATE THE BOWERS WITH BRIGHTLY
COLORED OBJECTS THEY FIND, LIKE BUTTONS,
BOTTLE CAPS, CLOTH, CLOTHESPINS, PAPER
CLIPS, STRING, AND GUM WRAPPERS. USING
CHARCOAL SOFTENED WITH SALIVA TO MAKE
BLACK PAINT AND CHEWED BERRIES TO MAKE
RED, BOWER BIRDS PAINT THE INSIDE
OF THEIR BOWERS.

IN THE MIDST OF BUILDING THE GRAND COULEE
DAM IN THE STATE OF WASHINGTON, ENGINEERS
WERE STYMIED BY THE PROBLEM OF THREAD-
ING A CABLE THROUGH A PIPELINE UNTIL AN
ANONYMOUS CAT SAVED THE DAY. HARNESSED
TO THE CABLE, THIS UNKNOWN HERO
CRAWLED THROUGH THE PIPELINE MAZE
TO SUCCESSFULLY FINISH THE JOB.

ELEPHANTS GO THROUGH SIX SETS OF TEETH IN
THEIR LIFETIME. WHEN THEIR LAST SET WEARS
DOWN, THEY CAN'T EAT ANYMORE,
SO THEY DIE.

A SNAIL BREATHES THROUGH ITS FOOT.

IT HAS BEEN ESTABLISHED THAT PEOPLE WHO OWN PETS LIVE LONGER, HAVE LESS STRESS, AND HAVE FEWER HEART ATTACKS.

FISH COUGH.

IN THE MIDDLE AGES, DURING THE FESTIVAL
OF SAINT JOHN, CATS WERE BURNED ALIVE
IN TOWN SQUARES.

ELEPHANTS SLEEP FOR ONLY 2 HOURS A DAY.

KOREA'S POSHINTANG - DOG MEAT SOUP -
IS A POPULAR ITEM ON SUMMERTIME MENUS,
DESPITE OUTCRY FROM OTHER NATIONS. THE
SOUP IS BELIEVED TO CURE SUMMER HEAT
AILMENTS, IMPROVE MALE VIRILITY,
AND IMPROVE WOMEN'S
COMPLEXIONS.

ANIMALS THAT LAY EGGS
DON'T HAVE BELLYBUTTONS.

IN THE 19TH CENTURY, KING HENRY I OF SAXONY
DECREED THAT THE FINE FOR KILLING A CAT
SHOULD BE SIXTY BUSHELS OF CORN.

MARIE ANTOINETTE'S DOG WAS
A SPANIEL NAMED THISBE.

MALE ANGLERFISH PHYSICALLY ATTACH
THEMSELVES TO FEMALES EARLY IN LIFE. THE
FEMALES CONTINUE TO GROW BUT THE MALES
DON'T. THE MALES ARE PARASITES. OVER TIME,
THEY LOSE MOST OF THEIR INNER ORGANS AND
DEPEND ON THE FEMALE'S BODIES TO SURVIVE.
TWO MALES MAY LIVE OFF ONE FEMALE.

THE LARGEST LEECH, WHICH LIVES IN
THE AMAZON JUNGLE, CAN REACH
ONE FOOT (30 CM) IN LENGTH.

IN RELATION TO THEIR BODY SIZE,
CATS HAVE THE LARGEST EYES OF ANY MAMMAL.

LEATHERBACK TURTLES' THROATS HAVE
SPINES THAT KEEP SLIPPERY PREY LIKE
JELLYFISH FROM SLIDING OUT
AND ESCAPING.

MOST PET OWNERS (94%) SAY THEIR PET
MAKES THEM SMILE MORE THAN ONCE A DAY.

A DRAGONFLY'S PENIS IS SHOVEL-SHAPED AT
THE END, TO SCOOP A RIVAL MALE'S SPERM
OUT OF THE FEMALE IT'S IMPREGNATING.

IN GENERAL, CATS LIVE LONGER THAN MOST
DOGS. AN AVERAGE LIFE SPAN MIGHT BE 12-14
YEARS. SOME CATS ARE REACHING 20 OR MORE.
A CAT'S LONGEVITY DEPENDS ON FEEDING,
GENETICS, ENVIRONMENT, VETERINARY CARE
AND SOME OTHER FACTORS. IT IS ALSO
IMPORTANT WHETHER OR NOT THE CAT LIVES
INDOORS OR IS ALLOWED OUTDOORS (OUTDOOR
CATS LIVE AN AVERAGE OF EIGHT YEARS).
THE GENERAL CONSENSUS IS THAT AT ABOUT
AGE 7 THE CAT CAN BE CONSIDERED AS
"MIDDLE-AGED" AND AT AGE
10 AND BEYOND – "OLD."

ELEPHANTS HAVE BEEN KNOWN TO
REMAIN STANDING AFTER THEY DIE.

PEKINGESE DOGS WERE SACRED TO
THE EMPERORS OF CHINA FOR MORE THAN
2,000 YEARS. THEY ARE ONE OF THE OLDEST
BREEDS OF DOGS IN THE WORLD.

CARMINE BEE-EATERS (A TYPE OF BIRD) BEGIN
THEIR NEST HOLES BY FLYING HEAD-FIRST INTO
THE DIRT TO MAKE A DENT. THEY LINE THEIR
NEST HOLES WITH THE REMAINS OF INSECTS
THEY EAT AND THEN THROW UP –
THE SMELL KEEPS THE RODENTS AWAY.

IN ANCIENT EGYPT, THE ENTIRE FAMILY WOULD
SHAVE THEIR EYEBROWS OFF AS A SIGN OF
MOURNING WHEN THE FAMILY CAT DIED.

WHEN AN ELEPHANT FAMILY MEMBER DIES,
THEY BURY THEM WITH TWIGS AND LEAVES
AND "CRY" FOR SEVERAL HOURS.

PRESIDENT FRANKLIN D. ROOSEVELT'S MOST
FAMOUS CANINE COMPANION WAS HIS
SCOTTISH TERRIER, FALA, WHO IS PART OF THE
ROOSEVELT MEMORIAL IN WASHINGTON, D.C.
BUT DURING ROOSEVELT'S 12 YEARS AND ONE
MONTH AS PRESIDENT, 11 DOGS LIVED IN THE
WHITE HOUSE. THEY INCLUDED A BULLMASTIFF,
TWO RED SETTERS, A RETRIEVER, A BULLDOG,
A LLEWELLIN SETTER, A SCOTCH TERRIER,
A GREAT DANE, A SHEEPDOG, AND A GERMAN
SHEPHERD WHO TRIED TO RIP THE PANTS
OFF THE BRITISH PRIME MINISTER.

ELEPHANT EARS CAN WEIGH OVER 100 LBS
(45 KG) AND BE 6 FT (1.8 M) ACROSS.
THEY USE THEM TO FAN AND COOL THEMSELVES.

IN ADDITION TO USING THEIR NOSES, CATS
CAN SMELL WITH THE JACOBSON'S ORGAN,
WHICH IS LOCATED IN THE UPPER
SURFACE OF THE MOUTH.

A PREGNANT GOLDFISH
IS CALLED A TWIT.

RESEARCHERS STUDYING WHAT DOGS LIKE TO EAT HAVE FOUND THAT THE APPETITE OF PET DOGS IS AFFECTED BY THE TASTE, TEXTURE AND SMELL OF THE FOOD, AND ALSO BY THE OWNERS' FOOD PREFERENCES, THEIR PERCEPTION OF THEIR PET, AND THE PHYSICAL ENVIRONMENT IN WHICH THE DOG IS EATING.

THE OPENING TO A CAVE WHERE A BEAR HIBERNATES IS ALWAYS ON THE NORTH SLOPE.

SCIENTISTS HAVE DISCOVERED THAT DOGS CAN SMELL THE PRESENCE OF AUTISM IN CHILDREN.

IN 1888, AN ESTIMATED 300,000 MUMMIFIED
CATS WERE FOUND AT BENI HASSAN, EGYPT.
THEY WERE SOLD AT $18.43 PER TON, AND
SHIPPED TO ENGLAND TO BE GROUND UP
AND USED FOR FERTILIZER.

THE BIGGEST FROG IN THE WORLD, THE GOLIATH
FROG, IS ALSO THE BEST HIGH JUMPER.
IT CAN LEAP 3 METERS INTO THE AIR.

IF YOUR CAT SNORES, OR ROLLS OVER
ON HIS BACK TO EXPOSE HIS BELLY,
IT MEANS HE TRUSTS YOU.

ZEBRAS CAN'T SEE THE COLOR ORANGE.

"SEIZURE ALERT" DOGS CAN ALERT THEIR
OWNERS UP TO AN HOUR BEFORE THE ONSET
OF AN EPILEPTIC SEIZURE.

THE ONLY DOG THAT DOESN'T HAVE
A PINK TONGUE IS THE CHOW.

IF LEFT TO HER OWN DEVICES, A FEMALE CAT
MAY HAVE 3-7 KITTENS EVERY FOUR MONTHS.
THIS IS WHY POPULATION CONTROL USING
SPAYING AND NEUTERING IS SO IMPORTANT.

PIGS CAN COVER A MILE IN 7.5 MINUTES
WHEN RUNNING AT TOP SPEED.

SEVENTY PERCENT OF PEOPLE SIGN THEIR
PET'S NAME ON GREETING CARDS AND 58%
INCLUDE THEIR PETS IN FAMILY AND HOLIDAY
PORTRAITS, ACCORDING TO A SURVEY DONE BY
THE AMERICAN ANIMAL HOSPITAL ASSOCIATION.

BY SOME UNKNOWN MEANS,
AN IGUANA CAN END ITS OWN LIFE.

IF A MALE CAT IS BOTH ORANGE AND BLACK IT
IS (BESIDES BEING EXTREMELY RARE) STERILE.
TO HAVE BOTH THE ORANGE AND THE BLACK
COAT COLORS, THE MALE CAT MUST HAVE ALL
OR PART OF BOTH FEMALE X CHROMOSOMES.
THIS UNUSUAL SEX CHROMOSOME COMBINATION
WILL RENDER THE MALE CAT STERILE.

A MULE WON'T SINK IN QUICKSAND
BUT A DONKEY WILL.

SMALL DOGS ARE RAPIDLY GAINING POPULAR-
ITY, ACCORDING TO AMERICAN KENNEL CLUB
REGISTRATION STATISTICS. THREE TOY BREEDS
ARE AMONG THE TOP 10 IN POPULARITY ON THE
MOST RECENT LIST: THE YORKSHIRE TERRIER,
CHIHUAHUA, AND SHIH TZU RANK 6TH, 9TH AND
10TH, RESPECTIVELY. A DECADE AGO, NO TOY
BREEDS WERE IN THE TOP 10.

A GOLDFISH HAS A MEMORY
SPAN OF 3 SECONDS.

HUMAN PAINKILLERS SUCH ACETAMINOPHEN
(TYLENOL) IS TOXIC TO CATS.

THIRTY-NINE PERCENT OF PET OWNERS SAY
THEY HAVE MORE PHOTOS OF THEIR PET THAN
OF THEIR SPOUSE OR SIGNIFICANT OTHER.
ONLY 21% SAY THEY HAVE MORE PHOTOS OF
THEIR SPOUSE OR SIGNIFICANT OTHER
THAN OF THEIR PET.

THE STARFISH IS ONE OF THE FEW ANIMALS THAT CAN TURN ITS STOMACH INSIDE OUT.

HAS YOUR CAT EVER BROUGHT ITS PREY TO YOUR DOOR? CATS DO THAT BECAUSE THEY REGARD THEIR OWNERS AS THEIR KITTENS. THE CATS ARE TEACHING THEIR "KITTENS" HOW TO HUNT BY BRINGING THEM FOOD. MOST PEOPLE AREN'T TOO DELIGHTED WHEN A PET BRINGS IN THEIR KILL. INSTEAD OF PUNISHING YOUR CAT, PRAISE IT FOR ITS EFFORTS, ACCEPT THE PREY, AND THEN SECRETLY THROW IT AWAY.

A JELLYFISH IS 95% WATER.

THE COMMON BELIEF THAT DOGS ARE
COLORBLIND IS FALSE. DOGS CAN SEE COLOR,
BUT IT ISN'T A COLOR SCHEME AS VIVID AS WE
SEE. THEY DISTINGUISH BETWEEN BLUE,
YELLOW, AND GREY, BUT PROBABLY DO NOT SEE
RED AND GREEN. THIS IS MUCH LIKE OUR
VISION AT TWILIGHT.

OWLS ARE ONE OF THE ONLY BIRDS
THAT CAN SEE THE COLOR BLUE.

FLORENCE NIGHTINGALE OWNED MORE
THAN 60 CATS IN HER LIFETIME.

THERE ARE MORE PLASTIC FLAMINGOS
IN THE U.S. THAN REAL ONES.

THE DACHSHUND IS ONE OF THE OLDEST DOG
BREEDS IN HISTORY (DATING BACK TO ANCIENT
EGYPT). THE NAME COMES FROM ONE OF ITS
EARLIEST USES - HUNTING BADGERS.
IN GERMAN, DACHS MEANS "BADGER,"
HUND IS "HOUND."

FROGS MAY BE HYPNOTISED BY PLACING THEM
ON THEIR BACK AND GENTLY STROKING
THEIR STOMACH.

ERNEST HEMINGWAY ONCE HAD AROUND
30 CATS AT HIS HOME IN HAVANA.

THE WORLD POPULATION OF CHICKENS IS
ABOUT EQUAL TO THE NUMBER OF PEOPLE.

PENGUINS CAN JUMP AS HIGH AS
6 FT (1.8 M) IN THE AIR.

THE FIRST DOG TO STAR IN AN AMERICAN MOVIE
WAS JEAN THE VITAGRAPH DOG, A BORDER
COLLIE MIX, WHO MADE HIS FIRST
FILM IN 1910.

EAR FURNISHINGS ARE THE HAIRS THAT
GROW INSIDE A CAT'S EARS.

MOST COWS GIVE MORE MILK WHEN
THEY LISTEN TO MUSIC.

THE FIRST DOGS TO HUNT IN PACKS AND THE
FIRST SMALL COMPANION BREEDS WERE
PROBABLY BRED IN ANCIENT CHINA. WRITTEN
RECORDS MORE THAN 4,000 YEARS OLD FROM
CHINA SHOW THAT DOG TRAINERS WERE HELD
IN HIGH ESTEEM AND THAT KENNEL MASTERS
RAISED AND LOOKED AFTER LARGE
NUMBERS OF DOGS.

MURPHY'S OIL SOAP IS THE CHEMICAL MOST COMMONLY USED TO CLEAN ELEPHANTS.

DECLAWING A CAT IS THE SAME AS CUTTING A HUMAN'S FINGERS OFF AT THE KNUCKLE. THERE ARE SEVERAL ALTERNATIVES TO A COMPLETE DECLAWING, INCLUDING TRIMMING OR A LESS RADICAL (THOUGH MORE INVOLVED) SURGERY TO REMOVE THE CLAWS. PREFERABLY, TRY TO TRAIN YOUR CAT TO USE A SCRATCHING POST.

WHEN OPOSSUMS ARE PLAYING "POSSUM," THEY ARE NOT PLAYING. THEY ACTUALLY PASS OUT FROM SHEER TERROR.

THE FIRST SEEING-EYE DOG WAS PRESENTED TO A BLIND PERSON ON APRIL 25, 1938.

EMUS AND KANGAROOS CAN'T WALK BACKWARDS, AND ARE ON THE AUSTRALIAN COAT OF ARMS FOR THAT REASON.

CONTRARY TO POPULAR BELIEF, THE CAT IS A SOCIAL ANIMAL. A PET CAT WILL RESPOND AND ANSWER TO SPEECH, AND SEEMS TO ENJOY HUMAN COMPANIONSHIP.

CROCODILES NEVER OUTGROW THE POOLS IN WHICH THEY LIVE. THAT MEANS THAT IF YOU PUT A BABY CROC IN AN AQUARIUM, IT WOULD BE LITTLE FOR THE REST OF ITS LIFE.

FROGS AND MOSQUITOES HAVE NO TEETH.

THE LARGEST AND THE SMALLEST DOGS TO LIVE
IN THE WHITE HOUSE WERE BOTH THERE DURING
THE TENURE OF PRESIDENT JAMES BUCHANAN.
THE PRESIDENT HAD A NEWFOUNDLAND NAMED
LARA. AND HIS NIECE, HARRIET LANE (WHO
SERVED AS WHITE HOUSE HOSTESS BECAUSE
THE PRESIDENT WAS UNMARRIED), HAD A TINY
TOY TERRIER NAMED PUNCH.

THE SMALLEST BREED OF DOG RECOGNIZED BY THE AMERICAN KENNEL CLUB IS THE CHIHUA-HUA, WHICH STANDS 6-9" (15-23 CM) AT THE TOP OF THE SHOULDERS AND WEIGHS 2-6 LBS (0.9-2.7 KG).
THE LARGEST IS THE IRISH WOLFHOUND, WHICH STANDS 30-35" (76-89 CM) AT THE TOP OF THE SHOULDERS AND WEIGHS 105-125 LBS (48-57 KG).

WHEN SNAKES ARE BORN WITH TWO HEADS, THEY FIGHT EACH OTHER FOR FOOD.

CATS, JUST LIKE PEOPLE, ARE SUBJECT TO ASTHMA. DUST, SMOKE, AND OTHER FORMS OF AIR POLLUTION IN YOUR CAT'S ENVIRONMENT CAN BE TROUBLESOME SOURCES OF IRRITATION.

PIGS ARE THE ONLY ANIMALS THAT WILL DRINK HARD LIQUOR VOLUNTARILY.

THE PUDU, A NATIVE OF CHILE'S TEMPERATE RAINFOREST, STANDS JUST 18" HIGH, MAKING IT THE WORLD'S SMALLEST DEER.

WHEN A FROG SWALLOWS A MEAL, HIS BULGY EYEBALLS WILL CLOSE AND GO DOWN INTO HIS HEAD. THIS IS BECAUSE THE EYEBALLS APPLY PRESSURE AND ACTUALLY PUSH A FROG'S MEAL DOWN HIS THROAT.

LEECHES ARE HERMAPHRODITES.

THE THEOBROMINE IN CHOCOLATE THAT STIMULATES THE CARDIAC AND NERVOUS SYSTEMS IS TOO MUCH FOR DOGS, ESPECIALLY SMALLER PUPS. A CHOCOLATE BAR IS POISONOUS TO DOGS AND CAN EVEN BE LETHAL.

MOST LIPSTICK CONTAINS FISH SCALES.

THERE ARE 701 TYPES OF PURE BREED DOGS.

IF ONE PLACES A TINY AMOUNT OF LIQUOR ON
A SCORPION, IT WILL INSTANTLY GO MAD
AND STING ITSELF TO DEATH.

CATS WITH LONG, LEAN BODIES ARE MORE LIKELY TO BE OUTGOING, AND MORE PROTECTIVE AND VOCAL THAN THOSE WITH A STOCKY BUILD.

THE SMALLEST OF THE RECOGNIZED DOG BREEDS, THE CHIHUAHUA, IS ALSO THE ONE THAT USUALLY LIVES THE LONGEST. NAMED FOR THE REGION OF MEXICO WHERE THEY WERE FIRST DISCOVERED IN THE MID-19TH CENTURY, THE CHIHUAHUA CAN LIVE ANYWHERE BETWEEN 11-18 YEARS.

MOOSE HAVE VERY POOR VISION. SOME HAVE
EVEN TRIED TO MATE WITH CARS.

THOUGH HUMAN NOSES HAVE AN IMPRESSIVE
5 MILLION OLFACTORY CELLS WITH WHICH TO
SMELL, SHEEPDOGS HAVE 220 MILLION,
ENABLING THEM TO SMELL 44 TIMES
BETTER THAN HUMANS.

AN OCTOPUS WILL EAT ITS OWN ARMS
IF IT GETS REALLY HUNGRY.

CATS USE MORE THAN 500 MUSCLES TO LEAP,
JUMP, AND SPRINT.

A SNAIL CAN SLEEP FOR THREE YEARS.

USING THEIR SWIVELLING EARS LIKE RADAR
DISHES, EXPERIMENTS HAVE SHOWN THAT
DOGS CAN LOCATE THE SOURCE OF A
SOUND IN 6/100THS OF A SECOND.

THE SMALL DARWIN'S FROG, WHICH LIVES IN
CHILE, NURTURES ITS YOUNG IN AN UNUSUAL
MANNER. AFTER THE FEMALE LAYS 30 OR SO
EGGS, THE MALE GUARDS THEM FOR TWO WEEKS
AND THEN SWALLOWS THE SURVIVING ONES.
THE OFFSPRING DEVELOP IN THE MALE'S VOCAL
POUCH UNTIL THEY'RE ABLE TO SURVIVE ON
THEIR OWN AND HOP OUT.

WALT DISNEY'S FAMILY DOG WAS NAMED LADY.
SHE WAS A POODLE.

CATS THAT LIVE TOGETHER SOMETIMES RUB
EACH OTHER'S HEADS TO SHOW THAT THEY HAVE
NO INTENTION OF FIGHTING. YOUNG CATS DO
THIS MORE OFTEN, ESPECIALLY WHEN
THEY ARE EXCITED.

A FEMALE OYSTER MAY PRODUCE 100 MILLION
YOUNG OVER HER LIFETIME

CATS TAKE BETWEEN 20-40
BREATHS PER MINUTE.

WHILE SMALL DOGS ARE GAINING IN
POPULARITY, THE TOP DOGS ARE STILL THE BIG
ONES. THE LABRADOR RETRIEVER,
GOLDEN RETRIEVER, AND GERMAN SHEPHERD
ARE FIRST, SECOND, AND THIRD ON LIST OF
THE AMERICAN KENNEL CLUB'S MOST
POPULAR BREEDS.

THE SPERM OF A MOUSE IS LONGER
THAN THE SPERM OF AN ELEPHANT.

THE WORD "ANIMAL" COMES FROM THE LATIN WORD
ANIMALE AND IS DERIVED FROM "ANIMA," MEANING
VITAL BREATH OR SOUL.

CATS STEP WITH BOTH LEFT LEGS, THEN BOTH
RIGHT LEGS WHEN THEY WALK OR RUN. THE
ONLY OTHER ANIMALS TO DO THIS ARE
THE GIRAFFE AND THE CAMEL.

RABBITS LOVE LIQUORICE – BUT IT IS VERY BAD
FOR THEM BECAUSE THEY CAN'T
DIGEST SUGARS.

WHO FIRST THOUGHT OF USING DOGS TO GUIDE
BLIND PEOPLE? AT THE END OF WORLD WAR I,
THE GERMAN GOVERNMENT TRAINED THE FIRST
GUIDE DOGS TO ASSIST BLIND WAR VETERANS.

THE SLEEPIEST MAMMALS ARE ARMADILLOS, SLOTHS AND OPOSSUMS. THEY SPEND 80% OF THEIR LIVES SLEEPING OR DOZING.

A CAT CAN JUMP AS MUCH AS SEVEN TIMES ITS HEIGHT AND CAN SPEND FIVE OR MORE HOURS A DAY GROOMING ITSELF.

A CAT CAN'T SEE DIRECTLY UNDER ITS NOSE. THIS IS WHY THE CAT CAN'T SEEM TO FIND TITBITS ON THE FLOOR.

THE PEREGRINE FALCON CAN SPOT ITS PREY
FROM MORE THAN 8 KM (5 MILES) AWAY.

A CAT USES ITS WHISKERS TO DETERMINE IF
A SPACE IS TOO SMALL TO SQUEEZE THROUGH.
THE WHISKERS ACT AS FEELERS OR ANTENNAE,
HELPING THE ANIMAL TO JUDGE THE PRECISE
WIDTH OF ANY PASSAGE.

ONE GOLDEN POISON-DART FROG COULD KILL
UP TO 1,500 PEOPLE WITH ITS POISON.

A CAT WILL ALMOST NEVER MEOW AT ANOTHER
CAT. CATS USE THIS SOUND FOR HUMANS.

SOME ANIMALS CAN GROW BACK PARTS OF
THEIR BODIES IF DAMAGED. STARFISH CAN
GROW NEW ARMS. SLOW-WORMS CAN GROW
BACK BROKEN-OFF TAILS. LIZARDS CAN GROW
NEW TAILS.

A CAT WILL NEVER BREAK A SWEAT BECAUSE
IT HAS NO SWEAT GLANDS.

MANY BIRDS MIGRATE, BUT THE ARCTIC TERN
TRAVELS FURTHEST. IT FLIES FROM THE ARCTIC
TO THE ANTARCTIC, AND BACK AGAIN,
A TRIP OF 20,000 MI (32.000 KM).

A CAT'S BRAIN IS MORE SIMILAR TO A
HUMAN'S BRAIN THAN THAT OF A DOG.

BLUEBOTTLE FLIES CAN SMELL MEAT
FROM DISTANCES 7 KM AWAY.

A CAT'S TONGUE IS SCRATCHY BECAUSE IT'S
LINED WITH PAPILLAE – TINY ELEVATED
BACKWARDS HOOKS THAT HELP TO
HOLD PREY IN PLACE.

A 15 YEAR-OLD CAT HAS PROBABLY SPENT
TEN YEARS OF ITS LIFE SLEEPING.

THE AMAZON JESUS CHRIST LIZARD
CAN RUN ACROSS WATER.

CATS MUST HAVE FAT IN THEIR DIET, BECAUSE
THEY CAN'T PRODUCE IT ON THEIR OWN.
NEVER FEED YOUR CAT DOG FOOD, BECAUSE
CATS NEED FIVE TIMES MORE PROTEIN
THAN DOGS DO.

AFTER BEING HANDLED, CATS LICK THEM-
SELVES TO SMOOTH THEIR FUR AND GET RID OF
THE HUMAN SMELL. LICKING IS ALSO THOUGHT
TO PRODUCE A CALMING EFFECT.

SNAKES CAN SEE THROUGH THEIR EYELIDS.

A FEMALE COD CAN LAY UP
TO 9 MILLION EGGS.

BOTH HUMANS AND CATS HAVE IDENTICAL
REGIONS IN THE BRAIN RESPONSIBLE
FOR EMOTION.

THERE IS AN ESTIMATED TOTAL OF ABOUT 1,100 SPECIES OF BATS WORLDWIDE, WHICH IS ABOUT 20% OF ALL CLASSIFIED MAMMAL SPECIES.

VULTURES SOMETIMES EAT SO MUCH THEY CAN'T TAKE OFF AGAIN.

THE BUMBLEBEE'S LATIN FAMILY NAME IS BOMBUS. THERE'S 250 KNOWN SPECIES AND THE INSECT IS KNOWN TO BE VERY SOCIAL. THEY LIVE IN THEIR OWN SOCIALITIES GOVERNED BY A QUEEN.

SOME GOATS CAN CLIMB TREES.

THE EMU'S TOP SPEED IS 31 MPH (50 KM/H) AND
THEY CAN GROW UP TIL 6.2 FT (190 CM) TALL.

PELICANS ARE VERY ATTENTIVE TO THEIR
YOUNG: WITNESS SAYS THAT THEY'VE SEEN
THE MOTHER PROVIDE HER OWN BLOOD WHEN
THERE'S NO FOOD AVAILABLE. OTHERS SAY
THAT PELICANS USED TO KILL THEIR YOUNG IN
THE SAME SITUATION BUT THEN WERE ABLE TO
BRING THEM BACK WITH THEIR BLOOD. BECAUSE
OF THESE BELIEFS THE PELICAN BECOME A
SYMBOL FOR THE SACRIFICE OF JESUS.

HOOVER, A HARBOR SEAL, WAS RESCUED AND GREW UP IN GEORGE AND ALICE SWALLOW'S BATHTUB (HE GOT HIS NAME BECAUSE THE FIRST THING HE ATE AT HIS FOSTER FAMILY WAS A PIECE OF A VACUUM CLEANER!). HE OUTGREW THE BATHTUB AND FINALLY MOVED TO NEW ENGLAND AQUARIUM. AT THE SWALLOW'S, HOOVER LEARNED HOW TO IMITATE HUMAN SPEECH. SO WHEN HE GOT TIRED OF THE VISITORS AT THE AQUARIUM HE WAS ABLE TO SAY: "GET OUTTA HERE!" THIS IS TRUE; YOU CAN WATCH HIM SAY IT ON YOUTUBE!

IF YOU WANT TO DO A PREGNANCY TEST ON YOUR PET LLAMA YOU SHOULD SHOW HER A MALE LLAMA. IF SHE SPITS ON THE MALE SHE IS PROBABLY PREGNANT.

THUMBELINA IS THE WORLD'S SMALLEST
HORSE. SHE'S ONLY 17" (43 CM) TALL
AND WEIGHTS 57 LBS (26 KG).

THE LADYBUG IS FAMOUS ALL OVER EUROPE
FOR BRINGING GOOD LUCK AND
NICE WEATHER.

ALL MAMMALS HAVE 7 NECK VERTEBRAS;
EVEN SO THE GIRAFFE.

THE SMALLEST DINOSAUR THAT HAS EXISTED
WAS NAMED MICROPACHYCEPHALOSAURUS. THE
NAME MEANS "SMALL THICK-HEADED LIZARD."
EVEN THOUGH IT WAS THE SMALLEST
DINOSAUR IT HAS THE LONGEST NAME.

THE FIRST ONE THAT MENTIONED REINDEERS IN
WRITING WAS JULIUS CAESAR. HE DESCRIBED
THE ANIMAL AS "AN OX SHAPED AS A STAG."
ALTHOUGH HE WAS CONVINCED THEY
ONLY HAD ONE HORN.

HIPPOS ARE NOT VERY SOCIAL ANIMALS.
THE ONLY SOCIAL BOND THAT HAS BEEN
OBSERVED IS THE ONE BETWEEN MOTHERS
AND DAUGHTERS.

SWANS ARE AMONG THE OLDEST BIRDS STILL
EXISTING. RECENT FOSSILS SHOW THAT
SIMILAR BIRDS EXISTED ALREADY IN THE
GEOLOGICAL EPOCH OF MIOCENE
(5.33 MILLION YEARS AGO).

SIBERIAN HAMSTERS ARE MONOGAMOUS; IF YOU
SEPARATE A COUPLE THEY MIGHT BECOME VERY
DEPRESSED, ESPECIALLY THE MALE. THE MALE
STARTS TO EAT TOO MUCH FOOD AND ACTUALLY
SHOW SOME DEPRESSION SYNDROMES THAT ARE
QUITE SIMILAR TO HUMAN DEPRESSION.

IF YOU EVER WONDERED WHY IT'S GOOD TO COUNT SHEEP TO GET TO SLEEP MORE EASILY, IT'S SUGGESTED THAT THE COUNTING SIMULATES RAPID EYE MOVEMENT, R.E.M, WHICH IS THE LIGHTEST STAGE OF SLEEP (AND THE SLEEPING STAGE WHERE WE DREAM).

THE LYNX IS THE ANIMAL THAT SEES WITHOUT BEING SEEN. IT IS OFTEN SAID TO KEEP THE SECRETS OF THE FOREST. IN MEDIEVAL TIMES PEOPLE BELIEVED THAT THE LYNX COULD PRODUCE GEMSTONES.

IS YOUR HOBBY STUDYING BUTTERFLIES? YOU
SHOULD KNOW THAT THE NEW TREND AROUND
NATURE-LOVING PEOPLE IS
DRAGONFLY WATCHING.

THE BULLDOG WAS BRED TO PERFORM AT
THE BLOOD GAME WITH THE SAME NAME:
AN ACT OF WORRYING AND TORMENTING BULLS.

HEDGEHOGS ARE USED FOR PEST CONTROL
IN PEOPLE'S GARDENS. THEY CAN EAT UP
TO 200 GRAMS (0.45 POUNDS) OF
INSECTS EVERY NIGHT.

THE WORD FOR GUINEA PIG IN DUTCH
MEANS "LITTLE PIG FROM THE SEA."